Chapter 1

Every little thing on the tray was flawlessly in place. It needed to be. There was a steaming pot of tea, honey and lemon wedges all perfectly set out on the shoelace doily. The elf lugging the tray looked concerned as she passed the ten foot Countdown Clock which was suspended over the rock archway. The clock checked out T- Minus One Hr.

She scampered down the ivy and also holly covered hallway passing a cluster of elves deep in discussion and briefly quit to appreciate one of the numerous brightly lit trees that lined the stone wall surfaces. She took a look at the hand embellished tree skirt with sequined angels playing heralds which reminded her of her days on the reindeer farm. "Get your head out of the clouds. Must not quit.

This is also vital," she claimed to herself as she regained her emphasis and also headed down the hallway.

As she turned the corner she was signed up with by an elf in his pushed white lab layer and also stethoscope and also a fairy in her scrubs as well as white cap from the connecting corridor who looked haggard as well as worn. Today had been a long day for everybody with the exception of Barnabas Crenshaw, that was hiding in the edge shadows in his gold head-elf one-piece suit, considering the current occasions. He flicked open his wrist watch video phone and his face was bathed in a blue white light. "Sherman to Moose and Squirrel. Now is the moment."

Gazing back at Barnabas was Helga Montclair. She was an extremely striking woman with black hair with grey streaks and also pet cat eye glasses, which mounted her mature looking face. "Understood. We will certainly exist in the morning," she replied with a really stern look.

" The touchdown pad will certainly be ready." Barnabas closed his watch video clip phone as well as smiled.

Chapter 2

The light was fading through the windows as Santa Claus fluffed his cushions and afterwards lay back down on his bed bring up the covers to conceal his blurry jammies. He evaluated his small, round glasses at the group that was bordering his bed. Before him stood Mrs. Claus, the elf in his white pushed laboratory layer, the elf in scrubs, as well as the elf with the tray of Santa's tea. "Please place the tray on the table and afterwards offer us some privacy," he stated to the fairy who dutifully took down the tray and left the area.

" So exactly how are we feeling this evening Mr. C?" the doctor asked.

" I've been much better, doc. I simply don't move as swiftly as I used to," Santa responded.

" We need a little bit much more light so I can analyze you."

" Fireplace much more light please," Santa asked, and the fire place instantly increased in breadth and depth to bath the space in extra light. "Thank you, fire place. Is that far better doc?"

" Now allow's take a look at you. At your age, you need to begin decreasing. Your high blood pressure has actually been through the roof recently."

" I've been telling him that for many years. You actually have me anxious," Mrs.

Claus added.

" Whatever will certainly be great, Mama. As you can see, an additional Christmas Eve went off splendidly."

" Open and also hold this under your tongue," the nurse said as she put a thermometer under Santa's tongue for a fast read. She counted thirty secs, eliminated the thermometer and stared at it momentarily. "His temp is typical, Physician."

" Have you been taking your drugs?" the physician asked. "Daily like clockwork," Santa responded.

" I make sure of that," Mrs. Claus claimed.

" I would claim take it easy or seriously you may take into consideration retiring," the physician claimed.

" You understand I can not do that. I've got to start servicing next year's plaything styles. I'll be great," Santa finished.

There was a peaceful knock at the door as Barnabas went into the area.

"Santa, there are a few points we require to talk about. Doc, is he mosting likely to be ok?"

" Nothing that some remainder would not treat."

" Thank you every person. I appreciate all your problem," Santa stated as he took a look around the room. "Mama, give us a couple of mins please."

The room was all of a sudden very vacant as well as quiet. The only sounds were the crackling as well as stands out of the wood in the fire place. "Barnabas, I know why you're here. You want me to select my successor. Have we found any kind of sensible candidates yet?"

Barnabas really did not take any time in answering. "Not really, Santa. The kindness keep an eye on has run completely dry, and there isn't any person that fits the criteria."

" If the kind deed display can not locate someone after that I'm afraid I just do not know what to do."

" I might have a solution," Barnabas said. Helga Montclair, Amalgamated Toys chief executive officer, is coming right here tomorrow to make a presentation."

" Why Amalgamated Toys? On Christmas day?

" They intend to reveal their dedication to making this help you and also every person. They are keeping an eye out for everybody's benefit."

" Are you certain about them?"

" Yes, Santa. They have an excellent reputation with the youngsters." "I will listen to what they say, however I do not wish to break custom."

" Customs are wonderful, yet in some cases it's far better to begin a brand-new one. Santa, please simply listen to what they have to state."

Chapter 3

The alarm on the bedside table clicked over to 7 AM, which was complied with by a radio DJ's voice, "Merry Christmas everybody." A little hand glided out from under the covers and also hit the alarm button extremely swiftly. The covers from the bed exploded into a rippling cloud as they were flung onto the floor. Molly Ann Thorsen, a precocious seven year old with long, curly hair, as well as using flannel jammies popped upright in her bed because today was Christmas Day. She jumped out of bed, flung her bedroom door open, as well as ran down the staircase heading straight for the Xmas tree in front of her in the living-room.

The tree lights shimmered in the morning serenity. Molly Ann paused to appreciate the packages embellished in their finest Christmas covering paper, bows and bows. She ran over to the tree as well as grabbed the very first gift. The tag read, "To Molly Ann From Santa." She grasped the present to her chest and smiled.

Chapter 4

The touchdown pads at the North Post were bordered by rows of blue lights and short paths. The elves had actually simply ended up cleaning off the snow with their shovels when Santa, Mrs. Claus and Barnabas climbed the staircases to fulfill their visitors who got on last technique. As they looked up a large sleigh drawn by four reindeer appeared the clouds. "Dasher, you are clear for landing on pad seventeen. Bring her in gently," roared from the speakers on a post. The sleigh made a perfect landing with only a mild skid on the ice. Inside were four passengers dressed entirely in white parkas, hats, handwear covers and scarves.

" Invite to the North Pole," Santa stated as he opened up the sleigh door as well as took his first guest's hand and led her down the actions to the snow-covered touchdown pad.

" Extremely great to fulfill you," Helga stated. "I have actually brought my right-hand man guy, High cliff Grable, CFO of Amalgamated, and our aides, Raphael as well as Nina."

" Ms. Montclair, this is Mrs. Claus, as well as you currently understand Barnabas." "Please call me Helga. It's an enjoyment to meet you," she stated as she

reached out as well as trembled Mrs. Claus's gloved hand.

" Call me CG," Cliff claimed as he stretched his distribute to shake Mrs. Claus's hand as well.

" Simply reveal us where to establish. It will not take us long," Helga claimed. "Then we can discuss their deal with each other," Barnabas stated.

Barnabas led the whole team to the meeting room with its neon hair chairs and pale environment-friendly seminar table. The blurry white walls enhanced the table and chairs. Helga quickly transferred to the head of the table complied with by Raphael holding a pile of papers.

" Greetings everyone. Raphael is going to pass out our proposal for you to evaluate, yet first please watch this short video clip," Helga said as the video clip screen decreased from the ceiling. The lights dimmed as the projector revived.

The video opened with very cosy shaped letters scrolling down the display. "Amalgamated Toys Presents The Santa Company." Helga appeared in the video clip looking very friendly and charming wearing very warm and also cheery colors with died black hair hiding her grey streaks.

" Amalgamated Toys is a company that takes care of our employees, the playthings, as well as particularly for the children worldwide." Next Helga became part of a very clean and also brilliantly lit storage facility with glossy conveyor belts filled with toys and satisfied workers in red Santa Company jumpsuits. "We have mosted likely to fantastic lengths to maintain our staff members delighted, as well as I understand we could do the exact same at the North Pole production center."

Now Santa, who had actually had sufficient of the video stood up and also disturbed the presentation. "I value the video and also all the documentation, as well as I make certain you will do a fantastic job. My primary concern is that the elves are taken care of." The video still played, but Nina turned the speak up.

CG stood in the middle of the projection display as the video clip remained to repeat him. "Santa, we totally understand your issue, and caring for the fairies is our top priority."

" With the power of Amalgamated Toys behind it, The Santa Company will certainly be an around the world shipment service for the playthings," Helga stated. Hearing this, Santa reluctantly took his seat.

" We intend to proceed your practice of good will and also joy, giving you assurance that the youngsters are left in our capable hands," CG stated.

" Consider it our method of thanking for all that you have actually corrected all these years," Helga said.

" We will update the sleigh shipment system with our fleet of new and improved Sleigh Master Four K cars," CG said.

" Santa, please count on page five in your handout and also you will certainly see the prototype," Raphael said.

Santa got hold of the pack of documents as well as scanned to web page five. On the page was a photo of an extremely contemporary, streamlined looking sleigh with all the bells and whistles. On the best side of the web page was a failure off all the features and upgrades for the sleigh consisting of a constructed in toaster, because Santa likes a treat while he is delivering presents. "Extremely nice," Santa stated.

" With these the distributions, we'll be much more reliable so the youngsters will get up on Xmas with their gifts under the tree. Bear in mind the wonderful ice tornado a few years back? Well these sleighs are equipped with ice busting tools so that even an ice tornado won't quit us. I know that Christmas was really harsh on you as well as rest assured the shipments will certainly make it through," CG said.

" Below's what we want to accomplish," Nina stated as she indicated the video clip which still played and also transformed the volume back up.

The video clip storyteller proceeded, "On Xmas morning the youngsters will be greeted by their Santa Company covered toys."

The video clip continued with a little girl in her jammies as she curved down and got her Santa Firm gift wrapped existing, resorted to the video camera and grinned. "Thanks, Santa Business," she said as the video went out.

" We will preserve the greatest standards and also use the clinical, oral as well as vision plan that you presently give to the fairies," Helga stated.

" At the forefront of The Santa Business will certainly be the Santa logo including your kindhearted smile," CG stated.

" So Santa, you can see we will certainly be able to ease your mind recognizing that your goodwill and cheer will certainly be performed all year," Helga claimed.

" As well as you will certainly be able to unwind as well as enjoy your gold years in peace," CG said.

Santa looked very ruminating as he touched his fingers on the table.

" Just consider all the downtime that you and also Mrs. C will certainly have. No more worries. No duties," Barnabas stated.

" I recognize, "Santa stated. "I'm not the young person I once was, and also there doesn't seem to be a sensible candidate to care for this remarkable area."

" That's where we are available in. We are the practical candidate to proceed your practices," Helga stated.

" We had our lawyer formulate a contract for you to look over," CG claimed. "Please give it to me," Santa claimed. "I'll think about it. This is a decision I.

can't make gently as well as need time to consider the ramifications.".

CG handed the contract, which was the size of a concrete block, to Santa that considered it with surprised eyes. "Thanks very much for coming all the way up here to make the discussion. I will offer you my answer shortly," Santa stated.

As the team got up as well as exited out the boardroom, Helga got Barnabas' arm, "Make sure he signs it! You will be rewarded handsomely.

Inform him this web page belongs to the bargain," she stated as she stuffed an eco-friendly web page into Barnabas' coat pocket.

Chapter 5.

Santa's workplace was brilliantly covered in all tones of red, gold and green from the floorings to the walls to the ceiling. Xmas threw up in this area. Santa went down the cinder block sized contract on the extra-large desk with a large thud and started to thumb with it. Santa's face was tinted with concern as Mrs. Claus sat in her shaking chair as well as weaved. With all his pacing, Barnabas put on a course in the red shag carpet.

" Barnabas, as Head Fairy, your input considerably matters considering that you've always had the most effective passion of the elves in your heart," Santa said.

" I've been guaranteed that everything will stay status. It's a win-win situation for every person," Barnabas claimed.

" How can you be so sure?" Santa asked.

" I've got the Fairy Rider right here guaranteeing their treatment," Barnabas stated as he took out the eco-friendly paper and swung it in the air. "It becomes part of the agreement," he claimed as he glided the web page onto all-time low of the agreement.

" Mom, what do you assume?" Santa asked.

" Before you sign anything I believe you need to have our legal representative look it over," she stated.

" That's not a negative concept. Barnabas, where is Stanislov?".

" He's out of touch visiting an unwell family member. We can send it to the contract specialists at Edward Langley Freemantle College to look over.".

" Papa, are you alright keeping that?".

" We can send it to them, and have it back soon," Barnabas claimed.' "They have the very best minds at E.L.F.U. If they claim it's alright after that I'm ok to.

sign. Ensure the Fairy Motorcyclist is attached Barnabas when you send it.".

Barnabas took the gigantic contract over to the dome designed transporter and also put it in the extremely open door. As he shut the door he slipped the eco-friendly web page Fairy Motorcyclist back right into his pocket and also closed the dome door. He after that pushed the eco-friendly switch. The dome was rapidly engulfed in a red light and the contract disappeared.

" I do miss my days at E.L.F.U.," Mrs. Claus claimed as she looked adoringly at Santa.

" Those were fantastic times weren't they, Dear?" Santa asked. The dome shone eco-friendly and vibrated as the contract came back.

Barnabas opened the dome as well as took out the agreement which had a note affixed.

" Beloved Santa, please feel free to authorize. Elf Marty," Barnabas checked out. He scanned the web pages as fast as he could.

" Any modifications?" Santa asked.

" No. Below's the E.L.F.U. Seal of Authorization," Barnabas said as he pulled out the signature page with the seal and also brought it to Santa.

" Are you prepared to authorize?" Mrs. Claus asked.

Santa checked out Mrs. Claus and after that to Barnabas as he reached for a pen. "I've obtained a fellow feeling about this." Santa scribbled his trademark by the large x on the web page.

Chapter 6.

Inside the wonderful hall all the fairies gathered to listen to Santa's huge news. Santa, Barnabas, Mrs. Claus, Helga, CG, Raphael and also Nina all gathered at the podium at the top of the two giant curved staircases covered in red carpets neglecting the collected crowd. Barnabas grabbed the microphone. "We have some very vital news to share with you before you head out on Christmas break. So without further so long I offer you Santa Claus.".

The elf group extremely supported and also praised as Santa approached the microphone. He looked a little nervous as he lastly got hold of the microphone, however before he spoke he had among his coughing fits. He removed his throat. "First I want to state that I really appreciate your hard work and also commitment to making Christmas so special." Santa stopped briefly while the elf crowd slapped as well as supported again. "As you understand, my wellness is causing me to slow down.".

" No it isn't Santa," among the fairies yelled.

" Thank you very much. You do not recognize how much I value that." Santa again cleared his throat. "I was presented with a chance that will profit everybody below. So I wish to let you recognize I have formally retired.".

The fairy crowd stared at Santa in shocked disbelief. Barnabas finally ordered the microphone and also sought to Santa. "Words can not convey how much I wish to thanks for all that you have actually provided for us for many years. You deserve this possibility to retire. Come on everybody, let's hear it for Santa Claus." Barnabas began slapping and also eventually the crowd slapped periodically till it was a surge of cheering as well as well wishes from the crowd.

" I am leaving you in the capable hands of The Santa Company," Santa said. "Please welcome Helga Montclair and also Cliff Grable.".

Helga approached the microphone, yet first quit to hug Santa. "I recognize change is frightening, however we welcome the difficulty to make this transition as smooth as feasible," she claimed.

CG slipped in front of Helga, "We anticipate working with all of you, so go have a terrific Christmas break, as well as we will see you when you return.

With the speeches over, the fairies snaked up the staircases to hug Santa and also claim their goodbyes. Numerous of the fairies visibly sobbed when they embraced.

Santa. After a huge selection of congratulations and also goodbyes, the crowd paid out and navigated their break leaving Santa and also Mrs. Claus alone.

Santa as well as Mrs. Claus strolled down the hallway holding hands as the platform faded behind them. "Papa, it's time for us to pack.".

" It's a lengthy journey to the South, as well as we have actually never ever taken this much stuff with us.".

" Well then, we require to load smartly. We can not fit as much as you do into.

your sleigh." They slowly strolled down the empty corridor, and all that can be heard was the echo of their footprints off the stone wall surfaces.

Chapter 7.

A heap of luggage and cleaner trunks obstructed the two story wood double doors in the front entryway corridor. A staff of concierge elves made fast workload up the Santabago, a modified Winnebago on skis and pulled by four reindeer. "Santa, the Santabago is stuffed and also prepared for your trip south.".

" Thanks, Nicholas," Santa claimed.

At this moment Helga, CG as well as Barnabas joined Santa as well as Mrs. Claus in the now vacant front access hall. "Helga as well as CG, I am trusting every little thing to you. Barnabas, please take good treatment of the fairies for me," Santa stated.

As Santa said his last farewells and hugged Barnabas, Nicholas opened the dual doors letting in the falling snow. "One last point," Santa said, "Helga Montclair, I give you the tricks to the North Pole." Santa handed Helga a 2 foot crystal secret which she happily approved.

" You will certainly not be dissatisfied," Helga claimed. "I'm depending on that," Santa stated.

Santa and also Mrs. Claus exited down the front staircases as well as crossed the snow covered ground to the stepstool by the door to the Santabago. Nicholas helped Mrs. Claus in, and also as Santa tipped up he reversed to take another take a look at the North Post. He looked tired and unfortunate. "Have a risk-free trip to the Crystal Palace," Nicholas claimed.

" We will, Nicholas," Santa claimed as he took the reins as well as glided into his seat.

He snapped the reins as well as the reindeer drew onward. "On Dasher, on Professional Dancer, on Prancer, on Vixen." The Santabago downed ahead and with reindeer power it took flight.

Helga observed this separation from the front hall window. She split a bad smile as she held the large crystal key close to her heart.

Chapter 8.

Santa watched out the window as the Santabago flew over the ice and snow listed below. It was snow regarding he might see. Lastly the radio revived. "Santa, this is Crystal Royal residence. You are clear for landing. Invite to the South Post," the air controller claimed. Heaven touchdown lights appeared from the ice as well as snow to note the path. At the end of the path the giant freight bay doors opened up on the side of the snow covered mountain. Santa slid the Santabago down for an extremely soft landing as well as moved the Santabago right into the cargo bay. There was a flurry of task as the elves got ready to welcome Santa and also Mrs. Claus. They created a straight line as the Santabago pulled up and also rolled out the red carpet for their visitors. "We are so grateful that you had a secure journey below," elf Spencer claimed. "The swimming pool is ready for you currently Santa if you wish to swim to kick back.".

" That is a superb concept. Do you mind Mama?".

" No, go right in advance. You know I won't have the ability to loosen up till all this luggage gets do away with," she stated. "Begin boys let's obtain relocating." She indicated the stack of travel suitcases, and the elves all made a beeline to get hold of a case.

Santa strutted down the ice blue hallway in his robe and slippers. Music was pumping from the earphones as he shimmied as well as drank to the songs. At the end of the hall was a steamed up door with gold lettering that read "Swimming pool". As he pushed open the door he felt the wave of cozy, moist air blow over him. The room was lit by skylights, given that the home windows were half covered up by snow, which blocked the natural light. Bubbles and steam dropped off the pool as Santa eliminated his bathrobe, exposing his swim trunks and storage tank top, and also put it on the chaise lounge. He roamed over to a poolside table that held a remote control. He grabbed the remote control as well as pressed the power switch. At the far end of the pool was a crystal slide with a steel plate on top. The steel plate opened up disclosing a round plastic tube that extended out into the snow. Within seconds a small flock of penguins obliterated the tube onto the slide and into the pool.

" Welcome back my buddies!" Santa said loudly as he did a cannon round right into the swimming pool..

Chapter 9

Their break mored than and the fairies started returning to the North Pole only to find the front door of Santa's Workshop secured, which was very unusual because it had actually never ever been secured before. The tiny crowd was really baffled. "Where's Barnabas?" elf Jilly asked.

Behind the door, gathered in the access hall, Helga, CG as well as Barnabas suggested. Helga and CG were no longer in their all white uniforms. Now they were clothed from head to toe in black.

" Look, if you get the fairies to comply on this relocation, after that you will continue to be the Head Fairy," Helga claimed.

" Otherwise you will certainly benched as well as relocated to cooking area detail," CG said.

" If it weren't for me you would not also be right here," Barnabas responded." "You're right. Just how does it feel to be the one that offered out Santa?" Helga

asked.

" I really did not market him out. I was seeking a method to assist him out," Barnabas claimed.

" Keep telling yourself that," Helga responded adhered to by a wicked laugh. "Let me chat with them first," Barnabas said.

Barnabas pressed open the doors and also slid bent on greet the crowd of elves who were expanding concerned. "Sorry for the delay. As you understand each time there are adjustments in monitoring points may not be exactly what you expect."

Helga as well as CG, who had actually expanded quick-tempered on their own, finally burst through the front doors.

" And you may not have expected me. Modifications remain in location. The biggest one is we are closing the North Post," she said.

" We are moving to an extra main area. The equipment right here is dated so we are moving to a cutting edge facility," CG said.

" Where are we going? This isn't best!" fairy Robert claimed. "What did Santa state?"

"Santa has no say right here anymore," Helga stated.

"We are mosting likely to a much more exotic area. I despise the cold.

The new plant is on the island of Topengo," CG claimed.

"We have taken the liberty of packing your points. Bring out the transport sleighs!" Helga shouted.

A loud rolling noise could be listened to coming from behind the back of the North Pole adhered to by puffs of black smoke. The engines of the sleighs rattled the windows as they slid out from behind the building led by marching guards clothed done in black. The sleighs resembled old yellow college buses drawn by reindeer. The buses dropped in front of the fairy group, and also the guards promptly herded the elves aboard. The fairies rapidly found that their baggage had currently been filled onto each sleigh.

Barnabas considered the scene in horror. "What have I done?" He and Raphael were the last ones loaded onto the sleighs.

The demented looking sleigh motorists got the reins and also fractured the whip. The reindeer began to draw the sleds till they reached a gallop, and also the sleighs took flight.

Fairy Jilly took a look around the sleigh to make certain she wasn't being seen. She slyly opened her wrist video clip phone and spoke quietly as a mouse right into it. "Santa, if you obtain this message we need your aid." She promptly closed her video phone as the sleigh guard looked her method..

Chapter 10

Helga and CG wasted no time in getting back to The Santa Company Headquarters in New York City. They walked in a tight formation as they pushed open the marketing department doors to be greeted by the marketing director, Caitlin, dressed in a cheery print dress that was a tiny bit short.

"Good to see you Caitlin. I hope you're planning on wowing us with your presentation," Helga said.

"We are hoping to make a big splash by the end of January," CG added.

"Great seeing you both," Caitlin said. "Follow me to the board room."

As they walked through the cubicles, the marketing department employees quickly ducked down out of sight. Helga stopped briefly to survey the room, which up until then had been bustling with activity. The cubicle workers plastered themselves to the walls of their cubicles, each praying that Helga wouldn't call out their name. She turned her head and continued to proceed into the boardroom.

The walls of the boardroom were covered in colorful Christmas advertising copy, and the marketing specialists stood at attention at the head of the drab brown conference table. Even the chairs were a drab shade of brown.

Caitlin pulled out her pointer. "With these strategies The Santa Company will have a worldwide presence. We are using a three pronged approach. Lance please proceed."

The suit wearing marketing specialist, Lance, stepped up and took over the meeting. "Step one is to set up promotions with our traditional retail outlets. We will set up year round Christmas departments."

Caitlin took her pointer and highlighted a spot on a chart on the wall. "We will change the toys in the stores to fit the season, for example a Fourth of July Santa." She pointed to a prototype of Santa dressed up as Uncle Sam which was already in its display box.

"The second step is a heavy TV advertising campaign to get consumers to feel the Christmas spirit year round," Lance said.

"Here is the commercial we will be running in all markets," Caitlin said as she picked up the remote and hit play.

On the flat screen TV the commercial ran. A smiling family was picking out their perfect Christmas tree. Next the family was eating a large Christmas dinner on a beautifully decorated table with the brightly lit Christmas tree in the background. The next scene was the family on Christmas morning in their pajamas, opening their gifts wrapped in The Santa Company gift paper. The picture faded to The Santa Company Logo. All of this was accompanied by a narrator.

"Christmas is that special time of year where good will and cheer fill the air. Don't you wish you could feel that year round? The Santa Company believes in keeping the Christmas spirit alive."

The video changed to a department store Christmas section with a little girl sitting on Santa's lap. An elf takes their picture as the narrator continues.

"Come into your local retailer to experience that elfin magic, and meet Santa without the long lines in one of our specialty Christmas departments. Bring your family and have a very Merry Christmas.

As the video faded, Caitlin turned on the lights.

"Incredible. Get these on the air immediately," Helga said.

"Our final approach will be online where you can order the gifts and have them delivered to your home," Lance said.

"What's so special about that?" CG asked.

"It is extra special when they are delivered by a reindeer and an elf," Caitlin said.

"Excellent!" Helga exclaimed.

Chapter 11

On the island of Topengo it was early morning as the transportation sleds made their landing on the make shift landing strips on the beach. The landings were rough as the elves were tossed about in the transportation sleds. Landing on sand wasn't as easy as landing on ice.

This was the first look the elves had of their new home, which was a horseshoe shaped island with a rocky volcano sitting in the middle of the green, dense jungle. As the elves disembarked, Leslie, the bubbly plant manager who couldn't be much older than twenty-five, greeted them. She was dressed all in black with her ponytail sticking out the back of her black ball cap and gripping her clipboard.

"Welcome to your new home. Don't go outside the fence. We cannot guarantee your safety from the toenayars if you do," she said.

"Time to get working. Get your things and head inside," Raphael said. "We have to get production up and running tonight."

"I'll make sure everything gets running smoothly," Barnabas said.

"I hope so," Leslie said. "Otherwise you won't be Head Elf much longer," she said with a smile.

The group of elves looked at the run-down factory which sat by the harbor and dock. It was not the gleaming factory that they had been promised.

Chapter 12

Inside the Crystal Palace Santa and Mrs. Claus faced a wall of TV monitors. Santa grabbed his chair and rolled over to the control panel. He flicked several buttons and levers, and the wall of TV monitors sprang to life.

"It's time I get caught up with everyone," Santa said.

"You needed the time off. See what's going on, and let me know if there is anything interesting happening. I have some knitting to work on," she said. "I'll be in my craft room if you need me." Mrs. Claus slipped out of the room, leaving Santa all alone at the control panel.

Santa grabbed the keyboard and typed away. He first pulled up the Santa Server, his email system, and logged in. A slew of emails immediately filled his in box. Several bright red urgent messages from elf Jilly awaited him. He clicked on the first one.

Elf Jilly appeared on the screen. "Santa, if you get this message we need your help." Santa wasn't sure what he was watching so he replayed the message again, Santa was confused and wasn't sure what this message meant.

While he was replaying the message again the screen flashed with an incoming live message. Santa clicked on the new message.

The video was elf Robert on a live feed, who was very dirty and disheveled. "Santa, I'm glad I reached you. You have to help us."

"What is going on?"

"They shut down the North Pole and moved everything to Topengo. The conditions are deplorable, and they have us working around the clock."

"Oh my gosh. I've been a fool."

"Have to go. Someone's coming." The video went black as elf Robert closed his watch video phone cutting the video feed.

"Mama come look at this."

Mrs. Claus entered the room carrying her current knitting project in progress. "I'm making you a sweater. Do you like the colors?" She asked.

"The colors are beautiful. Take a look," Santa said as he pointed to the screen and hit the play button on the keyboard.

"What is it?"

"A message from elf Jilly." The message asking for help replayed on the screen. "And elf Robert video phoned to say the North Pole is shut down and moved to Topengo. I don't even know where Topengo is," Santa said. "And I know where everywhere is!"

"Pull up the Elf Tracker. I'm not sure where Topengo is either," she said.

Santa hit more buttons on the control panel and up popped the Elf Tracking System on the screens. The video screens lit up showing a map of the world. There was a heavy concentration of green lights in the middle of the Pacific Ocean, lights at E.L.F.U. in Finland, several lights at the Crystal Palace in the South Pole, and two in Toledo, Ohio.

"Why are the majority of the elves here and not there?" Santa asked as he pointed to the clump on the video screen in the middle of the Pacific Ocean and not at the North Pole which was dark.

"Oh my my my. What will you do?"

"I don't know, but I need to get the elves back to the North Pole where they belong," Santa said as he opened his video phone. He placed the phone on the table facing himself. His concerned face appeared on the large screens in front of him. The red record light turned on

"To all my friends. I have let you down. I will do everything in my powers to make this right." He reached over and hit the send button.

"What now?" Mrs. Claus asked.

"I'm going there," Santa said pointing to the cluster of lights on the screen at Topengo.

Chapter 13

The factory bell screamed the end of the day. The tired and dirty elves dropped everything they had been working on, when all of their video phones rang at once. Santa's message played on all of their phones.

"Santa has heard us!" elf Jilly yelled.

"Our prayers have been answered," elf Robert said as he fell to his knees.

A party erupted on the factory floor as the elves danced around and hugged each other. Barnabas watched from an upper level gangway as a feeling of relief washed over him. But the dance party was cut short as the ground beneath their feet shook and everyone was thrown to the floor. The shaking subsided as dust fell from the ceiling rafters. Barnabas picked himself up off the gangway and brushed himself off. "Santa, please make it sooner than later," he said to himself.

Chapter 14

Santa flew the mini cooper sleigh over the open water. His only companion was Dasher, who was pulling the sleigh. He looked at the monitor and saw Topengo just ahead of him.

Suddenly the radio came to life.

"Topengo sky control to unidentified aircraft. Come in please. You have just popped up on our radar," the voice said.

Santa reached over for the microphone, "This is Santa Claus requesting permission to land."

"Santa? Please maintain your present altitude," the radar operator commanded.

In a state of panic the radar operator grabbed the microphone for the factory PA system, "Miss Montclair to the radar room. Miss Montclair to the radar room."

As the radar operator waited he could hear the heel clicks of Helga getting closer and closer until the door burst open.

"What is so important to drag me away from lunch? Helga screamed.

"Santa is on approach to the island," he said.

"What do you mean, 'on approach?'"

"See for yourself," as he pointed to the blink on the radar screen.

A voice came through the radio, "Is there anybody there?" Santa asked.

"Why Santa what an unexpected surprise. I just got back to oversee production," Helga said.

"I need your permission to land."

"I'm afraid that isn't going to happen. Too many company secrets here."

Surprised by Helga's response, Santa fumbled the microphone as it hit the floor. He scrambled and picked it back up. "I'm here to see the elves. You must let me land."

"Not today. Come back later."

Inside the radar office Helga pushed a lit yellow button. From outside there was a large boom which reverberated in the office.

Outside a large surface to air firework had been launched, heading directly for Santa's sleigh. The firework exploded, rocking the sleigh and bumping it off course.

Santa's radio came to life again, "How's that for turbulence? And there is more where that came from," Helga said.

"Are you kidding me" I'm only here to see the elves."

"The elves are fine. Please don't come back," Helga advised.

With the explosion, a group of elves ran outside to see what all the commotion was. The group jumped for joy upon seeing Santa's sleigh.

"See how he likes this," Helga said to the radar operator as her finger floated above a button titled Firestorm. She grabbed the microphone, "That was just a warning. I will give you five seconds to turn around and leave, Santa."

Santa looked at his radio as the countdown started.

"Five, four, three, two, one, last chance," Helga said.

Santa grabbed the reins and snapped them, signaling for Dasher to descend.

Inside the radar office, Helga pushed the Firestorm button. "Don't say I didn't warn you."

Multiple booms ripped through the warehouse as fireworks streaked from the ground aimed at Santa. The fireworks exploded around Santa's sleigh as Dasher pulled up and away. A row of fireworks exploded into the shape of multiple skull and crossbones, forming a wall. Santa jerked the reins, causing Dasher to pull the sleigh even further away from the wall of fireworks.

Santa, defeated, instructed Dasher, "Dasher, take us to Stanislov."

The elves fell to the ground and cried and screamed as the sleigh disappeared from sight.

Chapter 15

The trip took the rest of the night, but Santa's sleigh finally streaked across the clear blue sky over the city of Toledo, Ohio. "Dasher, prepare for stealth mode. I can't take any more surprises," frustrated Santa said as he flipped a switch on the dashboard. The sleigh smoked as a manmade cloud cover enveloped the sleigh.

From the ground a small child and her mother watched the one cloud fly the opposite direction of all the other clouds.

"Mama, look at that! Could it be Santa?"

"I doubt it sweetheart. It's an odd time of the year for him to be here," the mother said.

The cloud slowly descended to street level. Dasher and the sleigh emerged from the cloud as it landed. The sleigh parked in front of a grey, one story cinder block building with no real outstanding features. The sign over the door read Stanislov Law Office. The small girl pulled her mother over to Santa.

"May I give you my Christmas wish list now, or do I have to wait till Christmas?" she asked.

"This is better than Christmas. No one in my Christmas club is going to believe this. It is a pleasure meeting you, Santa!" the mother exclaimed.

"The pleasure is all mine," Santa said as he stepped out of the sleigh. He was now wearing his street clothes, which consisted of a bowler hat, a long tailed blue jacket, pin stripe pants, a white button down shirt, bow tie and spats. "Now what do you want for Christmas?"

As Santa bent over, the small girl cupped her hands around Santa's ear. She whispered her request so that her mother couldn't hear it.

The mother leaned in, but not to listen. "I want to thank you for my Betsy Wetsy doll from years ago. I really enjoyed my present," the mother said.

"You are welcome,"

"See mommy. Daddy is wrong. Santa is real like we keep telling him."

"Your father doesn't believe because he didn't get the Big Wheel he wanted for Christmas one year. No offense, Santa."

"None taken."

"Come on sweetheart, we need to let Santa get on with his day."

The small girl and her mother waved as they strolled down the street. Santa waved farewell and immediately went and pulled out a large cardboard box from the sleigh. He struggled to open the door and hold the box, but he managed to make it inside.

The receptionist stared at Santa as he set the cardboard box down on a small metal frame chair in the wood paneled lobby. “Look what the cat dragged in,” she said.

“Nice to see you again Rosie,” Santa said. Elf Rosie had worked as Stanislov’s receptionist for years and she was wearing her usual outfit of a black sweater, white collared shirt and a black skirt.

Rosie stood with her arms wide open and gave Santa a huge hug. Elf Stanislov honked his nose into a tissue, breaking up their hug. He was shorter and stockier than Santa, with grey hair and glasses, and about the same age.

“Rosie, please bring us some hot chocolate into my office,” Stanislov said, followed immediately by several deep coughs.

“Sure thing. I told you to get that cough looked at,” Rosie said. “Marshmallows, Santa?”

“You remembered!”

Stanlislov led Santa into his office. Surprisingly, it was a two story room with walls full of books, bright lights, colorful carpets and extremely cushy guest chairs in front of the ornate carved wood desk. Santa felt the heat from the fireplace as he set the cardboard box down on the desk.

“What a mess,” Stanislov said as he collapsed into his chair and coughed several more times. “Is this all the contract?” he said as he tapped the top of the box.

“Yes. There has to be a way to get the elves back and the North Pole.”

“I will look it over. I’m not sure I’ll find anything since E.L.F.U. gave their seal of approval, but I will check with them.”

“Find something.”

Their meeting got interrupted by the intercom on the desk. “Mr. Stanislov, your next appointment is here.” Rosie said.

“Send him in,” Stanislov said.

A very tall gentleman entered the hallowed sanctuary. He had blond hair, and you could tell he was of medium build, even with his winter clothes on. His wide smile brightened the room.

“This is Eric Thorsen. He is a contract specialist. Eric, this is Mr. Claus. I thought you two should meet,” Stanislov said.

"You wouldn't be any relation to the guy at the North Pole? You look like his spitting image," Eric said.

"That's because he is," Stanislov said.

"Wonderful to meet you," Santa said.

"Santa has been swindled. I need your help to break this contract," Stanislov said.

"My only concern is saving the elves. I tried to see them, but The Santa Company shot at my sleigh," Santa said.

"The elves are the priority," Stanislov said.

"If it weren't for Dasher, I would be fish bait," Santa said.

"I'll be glad to look it over," Eric said.

"How soon can you do that?" asked Santa.

"This evening. I'm picking up my family shortly to go to our church bake sale. You are more than welcome to come," Eric said.

"I would love to," Santa replied.

"Leave the Mini here. Get some rest. You've had a long day, and I've got even more help coming to look over the contract," Stanislov said.

Chapter 16

Eric and Santa pulled up in the family station wagon to a two story English Tudor home that was decorated in its Christmas best from the twinkle lights on the pitch of the roof to the garland wrapped around the wrought iron front railings.

They both hung their coats on the front entry coat tree.

"Honey, I'm home, and we have a guest," Eric yelled.

From the kitchen, Kelly popped out. "You should have called to let me know you were bringing someone with you," he said.

For a second Kelly froze in his tracks and stared at Santa. Molly Ann came running down the stairs and immediately jumped into Eric's waiting arms.

"Daddy!"

"Hi, Small Fry. How was your day?" Eric said as he bent down to one knee.

"It was wild! Aren't you Santa Claus?" she asked.

"Yes, the one and only," Santa said.

Molly Ann grabbed Eric and Santa's hands and dragged them both down the hallway into the kitchen. The kitchen counter was full of cakes wrapped in clear plastic with bows on top. Pots and pans overflowed the kitchen sink.

"Look what Pa Pop and I did!" Molly Ann said.

"It's the last of the cakes for the bake sale. Baking is an art," Kelly said.

"It sure looks and smells wonderful," Santa said.

"All right everyone we have to go. Time to get it together," Eric said.

"Why aren't you at the North Pole with the elves?" Molly Ann asked.

"They're not there anymore. I'm trying to fix that," Santa said.

"Where did they go? I thought they lived with you at the North Pole?" Molly Ann said.

"I used to live there, but since I retired I moved to the South Pole," Santa said.

"Santa's not supposed to retire. How are the elves going to make any toys if they're not there?" Molly Ann asked.

"Molly Ann, please be kind to our guest," Eric said.

"I was just asking," she said.

"She's got a point. I've got to get back to the North Pole to retrieve some items that will help me rescue the elves," Santa said.

"Right now, young lady, go grab your coat and make sure you put on your snow shoes," Kelly said.

Santa and the family climbed into the station wagon. Molly Ann buckled her seatbelt without even being asked, since she was trying to impress Santa. Eric and Kelly stacked the cakes into the rear cargo compartment of the station wagon.

"Are you kidding me? This man is crazy if he thinks he is Santa," Kelly whispered.

"Yes, it is him. Believe me. You just have to believe. You used to once," Eric said.

"We'll see. I don't like this," Kelly said.

Chapter 17

On a seemingly normal day Helga Montclair and Cliff Grable supervised the plant in Topengo.

"CG, where are we on production?" Helga asked.

"See for yourself," he replied.

With a sweeping arm CG pointed out the window to the fully loaded cargo ships in the harbor.

"The next set of ships are pulling out of the harbor as we speak," he said.

"Good. Good. Time to ramp it up. Call the help," Helga said.

CG reached over for the microphone on the desk. "Barnabas to the office," he said as his voice reverberated through the warehouse space. Barnabas, who was standing by the swiftly moving conveyer belt of toys raised his head. He quickly scurried through the conveyer belt isles and up the stairs to the office. He removed his hat as he stood at attention.

"Yes, Ms. Montcalair," he said.

"Barnabas, you need to motivate the elves. We are behind on our orders, and they need to be filled. Speed up the assembly line", she said.

"Yes, ma'am," he said.

"Our delivery deadlines must be met to keep our retailers happy," said CG.

Chapter 18

Tables of baked items lined one wall of the church rec space. The rows of tables with white table bed linen contained people talking, and also bookended by the basketball hoops on both ends. Sis Mary Katherine, a nun with incredibly thick glasses, as well as dressed in her complete routine, was greeting individuals at the front door as the Thorsen household and Santa came close to.

" Why Molly Ann, don't you look rather today," she stated. "Thanks, Sister," Molly Ann replied.

" Here are more cakes. As guaranteed, pineapple upside-down cake for you as well as German delicious chocolate for Dad Mike," Kelly said.

" Really great conference you, Sis," Santa stated. Santa transformed his head in the direction of Eric. "I'm mosting likely to call Mom. Excuse me." Santa left the team and also walked to the bleachers to call Mrs. Claus.

" Hi Papa. So excellent to see you!" she claimed. "I miss you," Santa claimed.

" I miss you too. Any progress on the elves?" she asked.

" No, not yet. I'm servicing it. Oh, he needs to quit that," he claimed. "Who requires to stop what?" she asked.

Santa was looking at a tiny team of children playing. A child was pulling the ponytails of among the girls. One of the ladies saw Santa and waved. Santa swung back.

" Advise me to update my mischievous listing. Jon Castillo simply drew Kim Stein's ponytail again," he claimed.

" That's not your fear anymore. Keep in mind, you retired." "I recognize, however idolizer hands are the Evil one's toys," he said.

" Don't stress. You have actually obtained me to keep you busy. Your honey-do list is getting pretty long."

" Prior to that checklist, I've reached find my substitute. What am I not seeing?" he asked.

" You'll discover that individual," she said.

Molly Ann walked her method over to Santa on the bleachers.

" Reached go. Love you, Mom." With that Santa hung up the video clip phone. "Who are you talking with?" Molly Ann asked.

" I was consulting with Mrs. Claus," he claimed.

" Is she feeding the reindeer? Is she with the fairies?"

" The reindeer are great. And no, she goes to residence today." "Did you know baby Jesus?" she asked.

" I never had the possibility, yet I make certain one of my predecessors understood him."

" I'm glad. No one must go without a present on Xmas."

In the meanwhile the row behind Santa as well as Molly Ann filled up with children wishing to speak to Santa as well as make their Xmas desires. Eric approached the team in the nick of time to listen to the end of Molly Ann and Santa's conversation.

" My views exactly. Time to order our seats. They're beginning dinner," Eric said.

Chapter 19

The family members left the church in their station wagon and headed house.

Molly Ann was out cold in her seat.

" Where do we begin?" Santa asked a little apprehensively.

" We require to take a good check out the agreement as well as see if there are any type of loopholes," Eric stated.

" Do you think that will function?" Santa asked.

" It's a place to begin. Otherwise, we require to formulate a plan of attack." "Exactly how do we do that?" Santa asked.

" See what The Santa Company's weak points are and also go after those. Can I ask you a concern?"

" Sure.".

" What does Xmas indicate to you?".

Santa thought momentarily. "Xmas is the sensation you obtain from friends and family. It's not about the sales in the shops.".

" You require to go public keeping that. Let individuals recognize how you truly feel.".

Upon their arrival house Kelly and Eric led Santa to his adorable and comfy space for the night. The bed was already denied for the night. Santa's suitcase sat by the foot of the bed.

" Santa, I wish the bed is comfortable sufficient for you," Kelly claimed. "Is Dasher risk-free?" Santa asked.

" Stanislov brought him over. It's a fenced backyard with lots of hay.

I've stowed away the sleigh hidden in the garage," Eric claimed. "Great. Is Molly Ann asleep?" Santa asked.

" Not yet. It's petition time if you wish to say goodnight.

Molly Ann was kneeling by her bed. The glow from the table light made her appearance angelic as Santa, Kelly and also Eric viewed her from the door.

" Precious God, please honor Father as well as Pop, and also aid Mr. Claus to rescue the fairies. He has done so a lot for everyone. Amen.".

Eric leaned over to Santa, "That's what I'm below for.".

Chapter 20.

Stanislov kept turning web page after page of the cinder block sized agreement sitting in front of him on his desk.

" I've mored than and over the agreement," he claimed. "As well as absolutely nothing?" Santa asked.

" I have actually considered hundreds of contracts for my clients. I don't even see the smallest way out," Eric said.

" When you authorized it you gave them control of everything," Stanislov said.

" But does that truly include my face? It's glued over whatever," Santa claimed. Santa got hold of the mug off of Stanislov's workdesk and also indicated his confront with the rosy red cheeks.

" No precedent exists to stop them from using it," Stanislov claimed. The meeting was disturbed by Rosie's voice on the intercom. "Mr. Stanislov, your visitor is below," she said.

" Send him in," Stanislov responded.

The door opened as well as in walked fairy Freddy who was really brilliant as well as chipper.

" Freddy, welcome," Stanislov claimed as he stood to hug him. "He's taken over for fairy Marty that did the original testimonial. Fairy Marty, with all his knowledge, has actually unfortunately passed on.".

" Marty was such a fantastic contract lawyer. E.L.F.U sent me to aid. I've obtained a duplicate of the agreement," Freddy said.

" I want to see if there is anything in the Elf Biker that can resolve this," Santa claimed.

Eric, Stanislov and also Freddy all looked to each other looking extremely baffled.

" What Elf Rider?" Stanislov asked.

" The Elf Rider. It specified the procedures for dealing with the elves," Santa stated.

" None people have actually ever seen it," Eric stated.

" It was on an eco-friendly sheet of paper. It's the only reason I signed the contract," Santa said.

" There is no green add-on to the contract," Stanislov said. "It was never consisted of in the last agreement," fairy Freddy stated.

" It simply could not have disappeared," Santa said.

" Or it was never ever consisted of to begin with. The last authorized copy of the contract did not include it," Freddy said.

" Considering that it is not there, it is not part of the contract. I'm sorry Santa," Stanislov said.

" Barnabas, how could you do this to me?" Santa asked.

Chapter 21.

Three elves, Ian, Thomas and also Robert evaluated the fence that formed their jail. The moon light shone brightly on the dense jungle simply on the other side of the chain link fence. They drew on the fencing, yet it really did not have any give to it.

" I truly don't believe what they say concerning the toenayars," fairy Ian claimed. "I have actually never seen one. I think they made it approximately scare us," fairy Robert said. "Now's the moment to make our break," elf Thomas stated.

" The security watercraft is just down the beach. If we can reach it we can get everyone off the island," fairy Ian stated.

Elf Robert took out a pair of bolt cutters. He reduced each web link in the fence till elf Thomas had the ability to bend the fencing back to create an escape hole.

Each elf squeezed through the opening and also slipped into the jungle.

The fairies rushed through the thick brush. The air was thick as well as hot as sweat poured down the fairies' faces as they battled with the thick hand fronds. All of a sudden a reduced scream froze them in their tracks.

" What was that?" elf Ian asked.

" I do not know, as well as I don't wish to learn," stated elf Robert.

From the bushes arised a serpent like dragon that was skimming across the sand like it was swimming. By the time the tail emerged the serpent was twenty feet from head to tail. The fairies iced up as the monster crossed the course in front of them and also disappeared back right into the jungle.

" Begin. Relocate!" fairy Thomas whispered.

The fairies made their way to the edge of the coastline and slowly drew back the hand fronds to make certain the coast was clear. They made a mad dash for the safety watercraft, however a toenayar moved in as well as blocked the path to the watercraft. The elves stopped dead in their tracks only to locate 2 even more toenayars had actually crawled their means onto the beach to block any kind of departure to either side.

" Prepare to safeguard yourselves!" fairy Ian screamed.

Elf Ian struck a Karate present. He pulled a black belt from his pocket and linked it around his head. Fairy Robert took out the bolt cutters as well as turned them backward and forward. Elf Thomas ordered a coconut from the coastline and threw it to and fro from hand to hand.

The first toenayar charged elf Thomas that wrestled with the pet. The beast opened his jaws and also discharge a dreadful scream. In that minute fairy.

Thomas was able to push the coconut down the animal's throat. The beast ran off choking and making sobbing audios.

The 2nd toenayar screamed and also charged elf Robert. Robert, that was spinning the bolt cutters very quickly till they formed a spinning star. Fairy Robert released the spinning star hitting the animal square on the head and knocking him out.

The final toenayar billed at elf Ian. Elf Ian quickly charged back as well as blurt his very own scream as he flew through the air. His karate kick landed directly under the monster's snout flipping the animal in reverse in the air.

When the beast landed he instantly went away right into the jungle. "The coastline is clear," elf Robert claimed.

The fairies completed their run to the dock where the protection boat was tied up. As they approached the watercraft they didn't see the journey cable. As the fairies broke the cord, it involved the catapult trigger causing an area of the dock to be rapidly launched upwards, expeling the elves in a spiral through the air and landing them in a web. The web ropes immediately pulled up, trapping the elves high off the ground.

" I believed you may try something such as this," Helga Montclair claimed as she emerged from the jungle with 4 guards equipped with livestock pushes.

" I hope this will not happen again," she said.

Chapter 22.

The cooking area gave off fresh baked bread as Kelly and Molly Ann completed placing the last of the filthy pans right into the dishwasher. Eric as well as Santa rested set down at the morning meal table drinking some tea as well as enjoying the still warm bread.

" I have actually reached go the North Post. The innovation I need exists. I don't have what I require to obtain onto Topengo," Santa said.

" I'll go with you," Eric said.

" Can I go? Please?" Molly Ann said.

" No sweetheart. You need to remain below," Kelly said. "It would be good for her," Eric said.

" Really?" Kelly responded.

" I'll put away the recipes after dinner for an entire month," Molly Ann provided.

" We will maintain her secure," Eric claimed. "Yes, Kelly I promise," Santa comforted.

As the night sunlight was setting, Eric drew the sleigh out of the garage. Santa currently had Dasher in his harness, and they hooked him as much as the Mini- Cooper sleigh.

" Make sure you pack your wintertime garments. It's a great deal chillier at the North Post than it is below," Santa said to Molly Ann, who was currently in her wintertime layer and hat. Kelly was bring a headscarf and also knapsack loaded with winter months garments and also a pair snacks.

" Please take care," Kelly implored.

" Sleigh travel is the most safe form of travel there is. We have never lost one yet," Santa said.

" See, Honey. It is much safer than taking the vehicle," Eric stated. Kelly came by and provided Eric a limited hug.

" I trust you. Be safe. Deal with our angel. Molly Ann, pay attention to your dad," Kelly claimed.

" Yes, Pa Pop," Molly Ann stated.

Eric took Molly Ann and also placed her into the rear. He buckled up her safety belt prior to he hopped into the front seat alongside Santa. Santa broke the reins. "On Dasher. Yah!" Santa screamed.

Dasher lunged onward increasing faster as well as faster. Within seconds the sleigh was off the ground and also heading north.

Chapter 23.

The metal barbecue tables were lined with tired fairies eating their difficult. The steel storage facility was a really gloomy location to be caught in. The fairies dipped their spoons in the grey tough just to allow the grey glop drop back right into its bowl.

" Barnabas, just how could you have allow this happen to us?" elf Robert asked. "We trusted you.".

" You trusted me? If it weren't for Santa we would not be in this mess.

Don't condemn me. Place the blame where it belongs ... on the huge male," Barnabas snapped back.

" Has anyone spoken with Santa?" elf Jilly asked. "He hasn't sent a message given that he stated he would certainly assist us.".

As she looked around the dining hall, all the elves shook their heads no. "Certainly he hasn't responded. He's living in the good life. I'm.

attempting to make the best of a negative situation right here, too," Barnabas said.

" Yeah, better for you, but except us," elf Jilly said. "You're simply selfish and think of just what's ideal for you.".

" If it weren't for me we would be functioning 24/7. I am trying, truthfully," Barnabas stated.

" I suggest you attempt harder," elf Jilly said.

Chapter 24.

Santa's sleigh flew over fields of blue ice as well as snow. In the distance the North Pole appeared, as well as Santa made his last preparations for landing.

" We will certainly get on the ground shortly. It's much easier when the elves are in the tower," Santa said.

" Is Mrs. Claus below?" Molly Ann asked.

" No, she is running the South Post while I'm gone. It's not an easy task maintaining the penguins in control.".

" Great! Do we reach see penguins here?" she asked. "No, they only live at the South Post," Eric responded. "That lives up right here?" she asked.

" Typically the fairies, Mrs. Claus, a lot of polar bears as well as I did," Santa stated.

" Polar bears are sooooo cute!" she said.

" Get ready to hold on. Dasher, bring us in slowly if you please.".

Dasher responded his head and also began the descent down. He brought the sled in for a smooth landing to a dark North Post.

" This is much more unbelievable than I ever before visualized," Eric claimed. "Not also shabby, huh?" Santa stated.

" Heck no!" Molly Ann said.

" The majority of people have a hard time relying on things they can't see." Santa said.

" That is what faith is all about," Eric claimed. "Precisely," Santa responded.

" When can we go in? I desire some warm delicious chocolate," Molly Ann said. "I had to turn in my tricks, yet there is a spare right below," Santa stated.

Santa checked out the lengthy icicles that hung off the front deck entrance eaves as well as began counting.

" One, two, 3, 4." Santa pointed to the 4th icicle. "Eric please grab that a person as well as shatter it on the ground,".

Eric reached up as well as got hold of the icicle and afterwards slammed it onto the front entrance floor. As he poked around the damaged icicle a crystal trick appeared in the smashed ice. Santa got the secret and also placed it in the lock. As he turned the vital the lock clicked. Santa transformed the handle as well as they got in.

" Where's the kitchen? I'm starving," Molly Ann said.

" It was a lengthy trip, Santa," Eric said.

" Come on. I'll repair something for us. It's terribly peaceful in below without the elves. I'm sure there is something left in the kitchen.".

As they went into the terrific hall, Molly Ann identified the spiral slide in the edge of the great hall from the second level balcony to the major floor. She let out a squeal as she added the stairs to the terrace. She ran to the top of the slide, grabbed the rails as well as released herself down the slide. The audio of her shouting resembled off the walls of the empty space.

" Seems like she is at house," Santa stated.

Chapter 25.

Helga paced backwards and forwards the rows of work areas in the marketing division of The Santa Company. Caitlin saw with a look of fear on her face while CG had a look of joy on his.

" I have actually just asked for one tiny point," Helga claimed.

" And that one small thing is the place of Santa. Why don't we have an answer?" CG asked.

" It's not like he has disappeared off the face of the earth, currently has he?" Helga asked.

" Santa has vanished without a trace. We are working on cause find him," Caitlin stated.

" Someone better obtain us the solution, and also we imply now!" CG shouted. "I do not intend to be assailed by him once again," Helga claimed.

One endure cube worker, a bookish looking woman, stood as well as elevated her hand.

" Yes?" Helga asked.

" Below is his Gaggle Coordinator page. It has his schedule on it," she stated.

She turned her laptop computer to Helga with Santa's Gaggle Organizer web page open. It reveals a photo of Santa and also his address at the South Post. A routine of his upcoming activities turned up.

" Lastly! Let's see," stated Helga.

Helga looked intently at the checklist of Santa's activities. The checklist included looks at the Ice Capades in Detroit, shop opening in Champaign, Illinois, Rodeo in Oklahoma City, 5K Marathon in Atlanta, volunteer time at church, browse through soup kitchen, as well as lastly, a look on Cope with Kelly.

" We'll begin right here," Helga stated as she indicated the Ice Capades in Detroit.

Chapter 26.

On Topengo the ground trembled and also the volcano gushed out heavy steam. Leslie looked exhausted as she stared at the volcano. She got the phone to telephone as the ground shook again.

" Ms. Montclair, we have a problem here," she said.

" I don't want to become aware of your troubles unless it is completion of the globe," Helga responded.

" We are experiencing more quakes and also it's freaking me out!" "Has it done any damage to the structures?".

" No, not yet.".

" Well call me when it does," as well as Helga hung up.

Leslie looked at her phone in awe as the dial tone buzzed. The ground shook once more, and Leslie ended up striking the floor. Elf Robert ranged from the storehouse panicked, as the ground lastly quit drinking.

" Miss Leslie, come fast. There's been a crash.".

They dashed into the storehouse, where a team of fairies has actually gathered around a large mechanical machine. They parted as Leslie and elf Robert showed up. There was an injured fairy lying on the ground with a cut as well as bloody leg. Barnabas was currently using bandages to the bleeding leg.

" What happened?" Leslie asked.

" He was working with top of the mangler when the quake struck. He dropped in and obtained trapped," fairy Robert stated.

" If it weren't for Barnabas cutting off the power there is no informing what would have taken place," fairy Jilly claimed.

" The medics are coming. He will certainly be okay," Barnabas claimed.

" Give thanks to God. He's lucky you were there to transform the power off," Leslie said.

" Yet he should not have actually been there in the first place," Barnabas said. The medics arrived and also began addressing the individual.

" Come on, everyone. The program's over. Take the remainder of the day off," Leslie said.

" If it weren't for me none of us would be right here. We would certainly still be protected at the North Pole," Barnabas stated.

" We are all attempting to reconcile a negative scenario. I miss my family members as well. He's going to be ok," Leslie said.

The paramedics grabbed the damaged elf and put him on the stretcher.

Chapter 27.

In the control room of the North Pole Santa pushed and drew items around until he discovered one that he was seeking. He held it up and after that gently placed it in his large red bag.

" Here's something we came for. The Portable Fairy Tracker. It's the only means I can track them out in the field," Santa said.

" What's the range of that?" Eric asked.

" As much as a mile. It will show me all the elves nearby.".

" Wonderful. Small fry ultimately dropped off to sleep. She is so thrilled to be below." "Good. I'm so pleased.".

" So this is the control center of your operations?".

" Yes, every little thing is controlled from here. You can see the manufacturing facility," and also Santa snapped a switch which turned on a video display showing the empty factory. "The stables." Santa flicked another switch which turned on another video clip screen revealing Dasher resting conveniently in the stable. "So it is simple to run the North Post.".

" If it is so simple why did you transform it over to The Santa Firm?" Santa strolled Eric down the hall to a space with the title, "Kind deeds.

Area." He pressed unlock to the dark area. With a flick of the switch a lighted world map was displayed on the gigantic 10 foot by 10 foot wall surface display looking similar to a vibrant Lightbright collection. From the facility of the gigantic monitor a radar arm turned clockwise.

" This is where I can see all the kindness on the planet." "What does this action Santa?".

" When a person gives of themselves easily a light will blip on the map.

There are not a great deal of good deeds taking place.

" So how did this obtain you to quit the North Post?".

" When one Santa retires, one more is picked. This display has actually directed every Santa to locate his substitute.".

" So you search for a concentration of light?" "Every kindness gives off a cosmic vibration." "So each light is a representation of that?".

" Precisely. But this time there wasn't one. I'm obtaining as well old to maintain waiting for the following substitute.".

" What a horrible scenario to be in.".

" And I didn't make the right decision.".

" Santa, you need to think that this will all get straightened." "I do. It will simply require time. Allow me show you the other area.".

Santa led Eric down the hall to another room with the title, "Negative Acts Area." Inside this room there was also a huge bank of monitors covering the wall with the globe map spread out throughout all the displays. As the radar arm swept the displays, multiple colored lights blinked on and also off.

" Each one of those lights represents a bad act. It became a disco, so the elves started having Saturday evening dancing events.".

" I might see how this would certainly obtain preventing.".

" I really did not mind the dancing events till the fairies began Elf Bowling.

That's where I drew the line. Too loud. One more quit.".

The last door Santa opened up was titled "R & d." The area contained metal racks full of equipment.

" What are we seeking?".

" 2 products. The Ice Manufacturer Ray Weapon TX and my Bubble Weapon.

Whatever we do is based upon ice, and also the island is extremely hot," Santa claimed. "The Bubble Weapon?".

" It supplies a momentary bubble of defense. I hope we don't need it, but I prefer to be risk-free than sorry.".

“Is this one of them?” Eric said as he pulled from the rack a shiny very retro looking ray gun that looked like it came out of a 1960’s science fiction double feature, labeled Ice Maker Ray Gun TX.

“Yes. And here’s the other one,” Santa said as he held the Bubble Gun over his head. “Let’s go.”

Chapter 28

Elf Thomas and also elf Harriet cleaned up the storehouse cooking area sinks, which teemed with dirty recipes. When elf Thomas activated the faucets, the water ran clear for a number of seconds before it turned filthy brown and also squirted water. Air blew with the faucet, splashing more dirty brown water.

" What the hell?" fairy Thomas stated. He transformed the tap off and then back on, yet it still sprayed unclean brownish water.

" Where's Barnabas" This is ridiculous. Will someone call Barnabas?" elf Harriet asked.

A 2nd later on a news from the PA system echoed throughout the storehouse. "Barnabas, you are required in the kitchen. Barnabas to the kitchen area."

Barnabas was sitting by the bedside of the hurt elf when he heard the announcement. "Seems like I have to go," Barnabas said to the hurt elf.

" Thank you for monitoring me," the injured elf claimed.

As Barnabas went into the cooking area, all he could scent was sulfur. As he checked out, brownish crud covered the recipes and also glasses.

" Add this to your listing of things that require to get fixed around here," elf Thomas stated.

" Yeah. This is simply gross," fairy Harriet said as she stood up a glass of brown water. "Take a whiff."

Barnabas leaned over and took a quick whiff and also jerked back extremely rapidly.

" Points just deviated for the even worse. Time to call Santa again," Barnabas stated.

Chapter 29

Eric as well as Santa came to the set of the morning TV show, "Good Day Toledo." Eric consulted with one of the manufacturers while Santa, in his best red match, stood in the wings. Ellie Konwin, the high, skinny, quite morning program host was chatting with her studio audience of thirty individuals seated in rows on steel chairs.

Eric signed up with Santa in the wings. "Remember the messages. You were tricked out of the North Post, as well as a result of that the fairies are in risk," he stated.

" Exactly how did we hop on right here?" Santa asked.

" They had an eleventh hour port open. We require to get public opinion on your side so you can get the North Pole back."

" Will this actually help me obtain it back?"

" Yes. You need to allow individuals know the facts to make sure that they can make an informed decision on buying with The Santa Company or otherwise."

" I understand."

" Cash is king to The Santa Company. No cash money, no Firm." "Will she be mild on me? I've never ever gotten on TV."

" Yes, the host is an old friend. She promised me she would behave." Santa paced to and fro. He could not stop wringing his hands.

The moment was lastly here as Ellie Konwin started Santa's introduction. "Please welcome my next visitor. He's the guy that claims to be the actual Santa Claus. Please welcome Santa!"

" Go get 'em," Eric said as he offered Santa a gentle push.

Santa waved to the clapping group as he worked his way to his seat on the Chapter next to Ellie.

" Welcome to Toledo. Just How does Santa Claus end up in Toledo, Ohio?" she asked.

" Well Ellie, I'm here to get words out that the fairies are in risk, as well as The Santa Business swiped the North Post from me."

" Why should our team believe you? You appear like a strolling advertisement for The Santa Company." Ellie indicated the video clip display behind Santa showing an advertisement for The Santa Company making use of Santa's face.

" I didn't recognize they would be utilizing my likeness when I authorized the agreement with them."

" So there is an agreement?"

" Yes, but my legal representative is filing documents as we talk with file a claim against The Santa Company for breach of contract."

" On what premises?" Ellie asked.

" For not securing the elves as guaranteed. They have placed them done in threat, and also I intend to see they are produced of injuries method."

" What makes you any type of various from the shopping center Santas presently on display throughout the nation?

" Due to the fact that I am the real Santa Claus. What can I do to verify it to you?" "I believe you Santa!" someone screamed from the audience.

" Thanks!" Santa said.

Ellie took a moment to assume it over before she reacted. "Because you know if everyone is rowdy or great, you have to recognize every person's name. Call each target market participant.

" So if I call them all, that will be enough proof?"

" Why not? Offer it a shot. Begin, target market, give him a little motivation. This will be a hoot."

The target market clapped noisally again.

Santa composed himself. "All right. Starting in the back row: Pete, Amy, Sandy." And Santa called all the workshop target market participants from start to finish. He also went on to name the members of the early morning show team. "On cam one is Shay. Your producer is Ted, and your audio lady is Niesa."

Ellie rested stunned momentarily. "That was incredible. Target market members, did he obtain your names right?"

The target market participants all shouted indeed as well as several drank their heads of course, however a lady in the back row raised her hand.

" Yes, you in the back row," Ellie said.

" He didn't obtain mine right. My name is Britney," she claimed.

"May I claim something?" Santa said.

" Please do," Ellie stated.

" Your name is Amy. Consult your moms and dads. You were

adopted correct?"

" Yes, I was. Exactly how did you understand that? Britney asked. "It's a gift. Do ask your parents," Santa stated.

" Any last words Santa?"

" Yes, Christmas is not what is found in a box. It's what you maintain in your hearts year round."

The audience blown away.

" Thank you for your time today Santa. Up following, 5 very easy recipes for quick suppers," Ellie completed.

" Green light," Ted the producer stated. "Did you get that on tape?" Ellie asked. "We sure did," Ted claimed.

" Place that on my page on our site. The more hits I get the more money they pay me."

Chapter 30

It was a very cool morning when Molly Ann as well as her close friend, Cassie, stepped off the yellow school bus. Dressed in their heaviest of wintertime coats, they lugged their publications and lunch bags. Several various other youngsters ran around the institution premises, tossing snowballs at each various other.

" Did you hear about Santa Claus?" Cassie asked. "What about him?" Molly Ann responded.

" He got on television below in Toledo today!"

" Yeah, I know. He's remaining at my house. My dad took him to the TV station."

" Truly?" Just how does your daddy recognize Santa?" "My papa works for Santa."

" OMG! I wish to meet him. Is your daddy a fairy?"

By now numerous of the various other kids eavesdropped on the conversation. Two of the children assumed it would be enjoyable to tease the women.

" Molly Ann still counts on Santa. I make certain you still rely on the Easter Rabbit as well!" said Matt. The various other youngsters chuckled.

" Santa shcmanta. Don't you understand where all your toys come from?" Steven stated. "They come from The Santa Firm."

" Steven Douglas, my playthings come from Santa and his fairies at the North Post," Molly Ann claimed. With That Said Molly Ann and also Cassie clutched their publications and also lunch bags as well as pushed passed the kids to enter the school.

Chapter 31

Inside the Topengo stockroom Helga paced in her workplace. She took her claw like fingernail and touched it on the home window and also beckoned Cliff right into her office.

" The Santa Firm was the most effective concept we ever before had," she stated. She reached down and also pulled out a brief-case from under her desk. When she opened it a stack of money befalled.

" Definitely!" Cliff claimed. Cliff got to down and also took out a briefcase from under his chair. When he opened it a heap of money fell out. Cliff giggled.

" We're raking in the cash," he claimed. "Let's make it rain," Helga claimed.

They each grabbed a thick pile of cash from the brief-cases and tossed it into the air. They danced around as the dollars fell back to the floor.

All of a sudden their dancing was disturbed by the ringing of Helga's phone. She got it as well as addressed it, but really did not say a word. She made an ashamed appearance as she hung up.

" Think that made a TV appearance today?

" Was it Queen Elizabeth? I hear she never ever offers meetings." "Santa did. They claimed it had not been on his schedule."

" How did that slide with the cracks?"

" He said he is intending on suing us. Within hours of his appearance our sales handed over. Xmas does not can be found in a box he claimed."

" The guy needs to be ruined." "I'll make sure that happens."

Chapter 32

The ice hockey field in downtown Detroit was festively decorated with banners on all sides. The banners review, "The Xmas Ice Capades, Sponsored By The Santa Business", and also "Invite Santa", all carried out in cheery holiday text as well as silver radiance.

Eric, Santa and Molly Ann strolled down the row of stairways to where the ice must be, yet rather there was a giant puddle on the sector flooring.

" I can't believe this. It's a washout," Eric said. "I am so sorry."

" I was anticipating satisfying the youngsters and also talking with journalism," Santa stated.

" It would have been a great chance to obtain the word out about saving the elves and also getting the North Post back," Eric said.

Curly haired field supervisor, John Sweeney, sheepishly made his means down the stairs to Santa, Eric as well as Molly Ann.

" Thanks for making the trip up here, yet it recommends absolutely nothing," he claimed. "Father, can I go sprinkle in the pool?" Molly Ann asked.

" No, you may not. You don't have your rubber galoshes on," Eric claimed. "There was a problem with the refrigeration units. We'll have to reschedule," John claimed.

" Should we hang around?" Eric asked.

" No. They're fixed, however won't freeze in time. I was really looking forward to seeing Santa in action," John stated.

" No ice after that?" Molly Ann asked.

" I have a means of addressing your trouble," Santa said.

" Actually? I do not see exactly how that is feasible, but I'm up for any suggestion," John stated.

" Just believe," Eric claimed.

" Mr. Sweeney, are my bags in the clothing space?" Santa asked. "Yes, they're backstage," he said.

Santa and the others made their way backstage to Santa's dressing room which had a gold star on the door with Santa between. Inside was a steel rolling rack with Santa's red fit hanging from it. Numerous open bags covered the couch, as well as Santa rooted with the old time rug bag.

" I know it's here. I'm pretty certain I loaded it," he said. "What are you searching for?" Molly Ann asked.

" Why my Ice Ray, certainly," Santa stated. "Ice Ray?" Molly Ann claimed.

" The North Post operates on ice modern technology. The fairies took care of to harness a few of it right into my ray weapon. Below it is," Santa said. Santa took out the Ice Manufacturer Ray Gun TX and also revealed it to Molly Ann.

" Great! Can I shoot it?" Molly Ann asked.

" It's very easy to use. See this switch?" Santa asked. "Yes.".

" You can either set it for ice or for snow. Which one do we require?" "Ice!".

" Correct. Allow's go make some ice.".

The team made their back to the stands, looking at the giant puddle of water on the arena flooring. Santa opened up the gate to the floor and also tipped gently right into the pool.

" Thankful I have my boots on," Santa said. "Are you sure this will work?" John asked. "If he claims it will, after that it will," Eric claimed.

" If you don't mind, can I have my internal video camera guy movie this?" John asked.

" Of course you can," Santa responded.

John ordered his walkie-talkie as well as phoned to the video camera control cubicle. "You prepared?" he asked.

The walkie-talkie snapped back, "We're filming currently. Proceed.".

John provided Santa the thumbs up. Santa stretched out his arms with the Ice Manufacturer Ray Gun TX and shot. Promptly an ice blue light created at the tip of the ray gun. Within a second, an ice blue beam shot out like a cannon. Anywhere the beam of light touched the water iced up promptly. Santa walked to the far end of the field floor as well as waved the Ice Maker Ray Weapon TX backward and forward freezing whatever in position. He made his way up the sector flooring, and also as he did he left behind an excellent ice sheet as if the Zamboni itself had actually come out and also cleansed the ice. As he reached the last corner he went back via the gate as well as off the ice.

" I do not intend to freeze myself to the ice," he stated. He made one last backward and forward activity with the Ice Manufacturer Ray

Weapon TX, and also the entire ice rink floor was covered in a gleaming sheet of ice.

Molly Ann competed onto the ice. "Make it snow!" she stated. "Would you such as the honor?".

" Yes, please.".

Santa handed the Ice Manufacturer Ray Weapon TX to Molly Ann. "Is that a good suggestion?" Eric asked.

" It is flawlessly risk-free. Go on. Just direct it up and also shoot," Santa claimed. "Oh, something initially." Santa flicked a switch on the side of the Ice Maker Ray Gun TX from Ice to Snow.

Molly Ann planted her feet, so as not to slip on the ice, and also directed the Ice Manufacturer Ray Gun TX up. She pulled the trigger as well as quickly a brilliant white light generated at the pointer of the Ice Manufacturer Ray Weapon TX. A second later on an umbrella designed light covered the entire ice rink and also a light snow dropped.

" You know my father is truly efficient his work. He looks after the tiny things just like me!" Molly Ann said.

" I'm not so tiny, and also he absolutely has actually taken good care of me," Santa claimed.

As snow gathered on her clothing as well as hair, Molly Ann hopped on the ice and made a snow angel.

The minute of fun was disrupted by John's walkie-talkie. "OK. I'll be right there," John stated. "Obtained ta go. The reps from The Santa Company are below.".

" Don't bother, we're currently below," said Helga in her hair coat and ruby necklace, as well as High cliff, wearing a Rolex watch, strolled down the stairways catching everyone by surprise.

" Wonderful to satisfy you," John said.

Helga aimed a boney finger with a huge ruby ring on it at Santa Claus. "Get him out of right here," she claimed. Santa switched off the Ice Maker Ray Weapon TX and also the glow from the umbrella light disappeared.

" I don't want you around anything that has to do with The Santa Business. Suing us! I'll squash you in court.".

" That will leave us without a Santa for the program," John stated.

" I do not care if you put an ape in a Santa Suit. He is refraining from doing this show," High cliff said.

" I'll obtain the fairies back as well as the North Post," Santa claimed. "See you in court.".

" Please have him removed from the facilities," Helga barked. "Santa, I'm so sorry. You don't deserve this, yet I'm going to have to.

ask you to leave," John claimed.

" We'll order or stuff as well as go out," Eric stated.

Chapter 33.

Helga shook her chair back and forth rather strongly as she beinged in the board space with the advertising department of The Santa Business. Caitlin stood ahead of the table in front of the video display.

" Despite the fact that you stopped Santa from executing, this still got out," Caitlin stated as she got the remote and struck play. A report showed up on the video clip display.

" Santa saves the day at the Ice Capades. He was able to refreeze the ice. Without him the show would not have actually gone on," the reporter stated. The news clip after that played the field internal video of Santa cold the ice. "Coverage live, I'm Heidi Fern for Network 5 information." Caitlin ordered the remote and also struck quit. The screen faded to black. Helga rested still for a minute as if she were trying to compose herself, but she lost that battle. She stood up as well as pushed her chair back to ensure that it banged against the wall surface.

" What are you individuals doing to stop him?" She shouted. "I see absolutely nothing!" She then slammed the table with her hand.

" Any individual? Anyone?" Cliff asked.

" Sales went down another twenty percent after this video went viral," Caitlin claimed.

" Someone better obtain me some responses. I mean currently! Stop him otherwise!

Don't come back right here until you can do that. Get out!" she yelled as she carried out a shoe and also tossed it at the door.

The advertising and marketing department members rapidly scattered out of the space, leaving High cliff as well as Caitlin unprotected.

" Get me the lawyers. I want to counter file a claim against the fat guy. I want to make his life unpleasant," she claimed.

Cliff and Caitlin both saw their chance to take off the space so they made their escape and also shut the door behind them.

Helga grabbed her chair as well as relaxed down. She pulled a letter from her pocket. The letterhead checked out Grand Cayman Bank. The letter detailed the account owner as Helga Montclair, and also the account number as XY74442. She got her phone as well as called.

" Accounting did you obtain the invoices I sent you today? They are to pay Consolidated Advertising.".

" Yes, ma'am," the accountancy department responded.

" Excellent. Below is the account number to wire the money to: XY74442.

Please send the money today.".

" XY74442. Yes, ma'am. The cash will certainly be wired today.".

" Thanks," Helga claimed as she hung up the phone and blurt a laugh.

Chapter 34.

Mrs. Claus was really worried as she examined the video clip e-mails for Santa. She punched a number of buttons to call Santa on his video phone.

" You have to go via your video e-mails," she claimed. "The number of?".

" A lot of! It is damaging my heart. You need to do something. Things are worsening for the elves.".

" I feel horrible, Mama. Keeping that protection system in position, I do not have sufficient guy power to get onto the island.".

" I understand, Papa. There is still time to get it fixed." "Mother, I need to go. The parade is starting.".

" Go out there and also sleigh them.".

The ceremony broadcasters huddled in their cubicle as the parade streamed in front of them. The bleachers across the street from them were packed with viewers in their ideal summer season endure this warm but windy day.

" Invite back to the yearly fourth of July Parade from New York City City," said Broadcaster Bill. "Martha it's a wonderful day below with the temperature in the 70's.".

" And also the entertainment will be incredible," Broadcaster Martha claimed. "Currently invite the New York College of Music marching band.".

The marching band moved with accuracy as they took spotlight in the parade path for their spotlight moment.

Santa viewed the ceremony from his sleigh which was put on hold from the Sponge Bob Square Trousers balloon, which likewise had a Christmas hat on. Four ceremony pedestrians held the ropes attached to all-time low of the sleigh. Eric was there on the ground under the balloon with his walkie talkie.

" Santa, are you OK up there? Eric asked. "Yes, but it is a little gusting up below.".

" Keep in mind when they interview you allow them understand you are here for the Nickelodeon Christmas in July Amazing.".

" I will. And afterwards can I tell them regarding the fairies?".

" Yes. I will certainly see you at the end. It's your time to go. Good luck.".

The parade walkers pulled on the trap unison to move the sleigh as well as the Sponge Bob Square Pants balloon into the ceremony procession. As the wind blew through the canyons of buildings, it drew several of the ceremony pedestrians off the ground and also bounced Santa around in the sleigh. The ceremony pedestrians obtained the balloon under control as well as headed down the ceremony path as Santa grinned and waved to the packed groups who lined the roads. The vending carts served everything from hotdogs to gelato on this warm summertime day.

The gelato cart was specifically hectic as people sought a way to cool off.

" Edgar, compose your mind," stated a dad to his son as he looked at the different tastes being provided from the ice cream vendor.

" I want rough roadway," Edgar said.

" We don't have that," claimed the cart supplier. "Select another taste." "I desire rough road!" Edgar shouted.

" Edgar, please pick another taste. He does not have that," stated his annoyed papa.

Edgar stamped his feet and also started kicking points. He also kicked the square blocks before the cart wheels into the road.

" Begin youngster. What do you want? Can not you see you're holding up the line," the supplier said.

" Do you have waffle cones?" the daddy asked.

" Allow me look." The vendor then bent over to examine packages he had actually piled behind the cart.

At the very same time the dad ordered Edgar by the shoulders. "Be nice," he stated.

Santa as well as the Sponge Bob Square Pants balloon approached the corner where the ice cream cart was resting. A large gust of wind caught the ice cream cart umbrella, causing the cart to roll down the sloped curb. The cart bent unmanageable down the road. It took care of to knock down all 4 of the parade pedestrians holding the balloon ropes like a bowling round overruling bowling pins. Because instantaneous Santa and also the Sponge Bob Square Trousers balloon were released.

" Whoa!" Santa said loudly as he was thrown onto the flooring of the sleigh.

The parade walkers tried to recuperate, and also started chasing Santa as well as the balloon as it jumped and also skipped off of the structures lining the road. Santa and the balloon increased as they were both blown down a backstreet and off the parade path.

At that moment Helga was exiting the home office of the Santa Firm as Santa and also Sponge Bob went blowing past her.

" Good morning Helga!" Santa shouted from the sleigh.

" What the hell?" Helga stated to herself.

Inside the sleigh Santa was able to gain back some calmness and also grabbed the walkie talkie.

" Eric been available in. Eric come in," Santa said.

Eric's voice could be learnt through the walkie talkie, "Are you ok?" "Until now. This is a little bumpier than my typical flights. Obtain me out of here!".

" They're tracking you now," Eric reacted.

The sleigh and also balloon flashed of the structure canyon as well as removed over Battery Park and also were headed over the Hudson River. The wind was blowing the balloon on a direct collision course with the Statue of Liberty. The visitors in the crown monitoring deck of the Sculpture of Liberty scrambled as it emerged that the sleigh and also balloon went to a direct hit with the Statue. Sponge Bob was lanced by among the rays of crown from the Sculpture causing it to decrease and head straight to the pedestal listed below. As the sleigh bounced on the ground, Santa was ejected and also jumped on the hot concrete.

" I'm as well old for this," Santa stated..

Chapter 35

Kelly as well as Molly Ann pressed their shopping cart down the grain aisle of the local Piggly Wiggly grocery store. In the cart sat a heap of grocery stores as well as Kelly's shoulder bag.

" Pop, can we please have this? It is my favored."

" You just like it for all the sugar. Remember too much sugar will rot your teeth."

As Kelly as well as Molly Ann researched the numerous boxes of grain a strange man as well as his kid approached them.

" Isn't your hubby aiding the supposed Santa Claus?" the male asked.
"Yes, he is assisting the actual Santa Claus," Kelly reacted.

" Well he needs to quit it. He is puzzling my kid and also spoiling his Christmas," the male claimed.

" Santa is at the shopping mall now. He's the actual Santa. Not that phony one. Father, make them stop," the boy claimed.

By now a team of buyers stopped as well as gazed as the conversation proceeded.

" See what you are placing him via? He does not know what to believe. Your husband needs to be ashamed," the male said.

" I'm sorry you really feel in this way. My other half is just attempting to be handy.

And Santa is trying to get the North Post back," Kelly claimed.

" After that he should not have actually offered it up in the first place. Come on child, we need to go." As he walked away he intentionally bumped the cart.

Kelly's face drained of shade as the various other buyers paid out. "Santa didn't do anything wrong," Molly Ann said.

" Some people do not see it in this way. We need to go now," Kelly said.

As they walked up the aisle they pressed their cart by the publication rack and also on the cover of Star Manufacturer Publication was an image of Santa Claus. The headline read, "The Actual Thing?"

As Kelly and Molly Ann entered the mud area of their home they both removed their footwear. Kelly was certainly worried. Santa and also Eric aided by placing the grocery store bags on the kitchen counter.

" We were accosted by a very upset parent who was mad at Santa," Kelly stated.

" Are you both OK?" Eric asked.

" Yes, Father. Some suggest aggressive guy entered Pa Pop's face," Molly Ann said.

" I do not indicate to trigger any problems," Santa stated.

" Typically it's just whispers, however this individual remained in my face," Kelly said.

" I desire this fixed as long as you do. I'm sorry people are taking their rage out on you," Santa said.

" I value that," Kelly claimed.

Chapter 36

In the attorney's office Helga and also CG came close to the 3 lawyers, who stood at a giant timber workdesk with a wall of books behind them. They had actually slicked back salt as well as pepper hair, as well as all dressed in identical matches. The lawyers seemed to function as one being.

" Helga, it is so wonderful to see you," Attorney # 1 stated. "CG, we rejoice you're right here," Legal representative # 2 claimed. "We have actually seen the claim," Layer # 3 said.

" Do I need to be stressed over this?" Helga asked.

" We didn't spend all this moment and also money into this company to watch it obtain sidetracked by some depleted has-been," Cliff stated.

" We pay you great cash, so you 'd much better give me some answers!" Helga demanded.

" It is effectively created, because we created it," Legal representative # 2 said. "We do not believe you have a trouble," Attorney # 1 claimed.

" His whole instance hinges on the Fairy Cyclist which was never included in the agreement," Legal representative # 3 said.

" Thanks Barnabas," Helga said.

" He was sold out by his Head Elf so if he wishes to file a claim against someone, pursue him," Legal representative # 2 stated.

" Great. File a counter fit against Santa. He has no money, so allow's prevent him from emerging as himself," Helga stated.

Chapter 37

A few days later Helga strolled down the courthouse steps with her three attorneys as well as CG in tow. She was holding a handful of paperwork in her hands. She and her group had submitted the countersuit against Santa.

" I wish Santa likes our response," Helga said,

" We have him buried in paperwork that will certainly take months for his group to survive," Attorney # 2 claimed.

" What do you suggest?" Helga asked.

" With that much to go through, this case could take months to head to court," Attorney # 1 claimed.

" Oh geez," CG stated.

" That's not soon enough. I desire him humiliated earlier than later," Helga stated.

" What do you recommend we do?" CG asked.

" I have a plan to speed this up. Obtain me advertising and marketing," Helga stated.

Chapter 38

The Praise indication flashed to the workshop audience as Kelly Ripa and her co-host, Neil Patrick Harris bantered backward and forward.

The Chapter supervisor did a countdown, "Four, 3, two, one" as well as pointed to Kelly.

" Our following guest has been making viral waves with his video clips on Bloobtube. Please welcome Santa Claus.

The audience stood up and applauded Santa as he went into the workshop and also took his seat.

" What brings you to New York?" Neil asked.

" I desire people to know that the elves remain in threat. I understand some individuals do not trust me, yet they require to think me."

" What risk? Aren't they operating at the North Pole?" Kelly asked. "No, they work on an island in the Pacific Sea in awful conditions,"

Santa stated.

" What can we do?" Kelly asked.

" Obtain The Santa Business to recognize their promise to care for the fairies."

" Exactly how do you feel The Santa Company is ruining, I imply running Christmas?" Neil asked.

" My mother raised me never ever to talk ill of anyone. She was polite that way," Santa said.

" Well, I don't understand if this is an excellent surprise for you any longer," Kelly stated.

" Ladies and also gents, please welcome Helga Montclair and also Cliff Grable from The Santa Company," Neil stated as he introduced the pair.

Helga and CG walked their means across the stage to their chairs opposite Santa.

" What have you done to the Elves?" Santa asked.

" The elves are great," Helga claimed. "Toys are being provided worldwide as we speak."

" That's not what they tell me," Santa claimed.

" There's always one dissatisfied worker," Helga claimed.

" Santa, we want to thanks for keeping the spirit of Xmas alive and well," CG said.

" And also we have actually generated the best way to thank. We have something for you. Bring it on out," Helga stated.

A boy putting on a blue match marched from behind the drapes lugging a blue envelope. He crossed the stage and also handed Santa the blue envelope.

" What is this?" Santa asked.

The boy stated, "In behalf of the city of New York, consider yourself offered in the case of Santa Claus versus The Santa Company."

" I'm served?" Santa claimed. Santa opened up the envelope as well as swiftly checked its materials.

" Yes, we are suing you to ensure that you can't appear as Santa Claus," Helga said.

" Just how is that possible?" Santa asked. "We possess your picture," Helga claimed.

" Santa, we had no idea," Kelly claimed. "We were informed it was mosting likely to be a thank you present."

" I recognize someone who is obtaining a swelling of coal in their equipping," Neil claimed.

Eric entered from the wing of the Chapter and also grabbed Santa and also pulled him off stage.

Helga cackled as Santa got away the Chapter.

Chapter 39

It was brilliant in the institution hallway as Molly Ann and also Cassie walked to their homeroom and also gripped their publications in their arms.

" I obtained Mrs. Phender for homeroom this year," Molly Ann claimed. "I heard she is really nice."

" I got Mrs. Springer," Cassie claimed. "She has dreadful breath." And also both women chuckled.

As they turned the hall corner they were come close to by Matt and also Steven. "If it isn't little Miss Christmas," Steven said.

" Just neglect them," Molly Ann stated. "Little young boys will be little young boys." "So just how is your life with San-tee Claus?" Matt asked.

" For your details, it is fantastic," Molly Ann reacted. "I've seen a great deal of areas, consisting of the North Pole,"

Both the kids took a look at each other and laughed.

" The North Post?" Steven said. "Did you reach play with Rudolph? Did the little elves make you a bunch of cookies?"

" Did you consume eggnog and also make toys?" Matt asked.

" There was no one there," Molly Ann replied. "It was really silent." "They heard you were coming so they all escaped to get away from

your cooties," Steven said.

" Molly Ann has cooties!" Matt screamed as loud as he could.

" Extremely fully grown," Cassie stated. "Begin Molly Ann, we're leaving." Both the children chuckled and also pushed each other happily, however as they did,

Matt bumped Molly Ann as she turned to leave. She shed her equilibrium and also tumbled down the staircase, and wound up in a heap at the bottom.

" Molly Ann!" Cassie yelled. As well as certainly, the little young boys ran.

Chapter 40

Eric, Kelly as well as Santa Claus burst with the doors of the medical facility as well as came close to the nurse with a needle nose at the registered nurse's station. She was active cleaning her red hair out of her eyes as she read a patient's graph.

" Where's my little girl, Molly Ann?" Kelly asked.

" They just brought her in. She is in room five," Registered nurse Barbra said. "Who's going to fill in her documentation?" she asked as she held up a clipboard with documents attached. Kelly looked at the clipboard and then took off down the corridor.

" I'll fill it out," Eric said as he got hold of the clipboard from the registered nurse. "Do you have insurance?" Registered nurse Barbra asked.

Molly Ann was pushing the bed with a bandage wrapped around her head The physician was already looking her over.

" Pa Pop!" Molly Ann claimed as Kelly entered the space as well as gave her a huge hug.

" Child, are you OK? Kelly claimed. "I am so sorry this took place." "She'll be fine," Medical professional Mason said. "She just obtained a bump on the head.

and also a couple of scrapes. It could have been much even worse." "Will she be able to go home?" Kelly asked.

" Not today." Physician Mason responded. "With a head injury we wish to maintain her overnight for observation."

" Pa Pop, where's Dad?" Molly Ann asked. "Right below," Eric stated slipping into the room. "Father!" Eric offered Molly Ann a huge hug.

" That's rather a try to find you, Little Fry," Eric said. "It doesn't injured. Can I go home currently?"

" Honey you heard what the physician said. I'll be with you all night," Kelly claimed.

" What took place, Molly Ann?" Santa asked.

" Some boys were teasing me for counting on you. After that they stated I had cooties," Molly Ann responded.

" She took a tumble down a staircase," Doctor Mason said. "Exactly how horrible," Santa said.

" Eric, may I talk to you in the corridor?" Kelly asked.

Kelly got Eric's hand and they headed out right into the corridor to an empty place where they had some personal privacy.

" Did you believe he would really obtain the North Post back?" Kelly asked. "Our little girl is existing there in a medical facility bed."

" I never thought it would reach this."

" That's the trouble. You never ever think. You need to do away with your partner and begin focusing on your family members and your various other customers."

" I have a task to Santa," Eric stated. "You recognize when I start collaborating with a customer I see their project completely with."

" Well you would certainly much better think of that. This Papa Bear is pissed, and also if you do not dump your customer, "I'm taking Molly Ann to my moms and dads for her own safety."

" You do not mean that," Eric claimed. "Yes I do. Get rid of Santa otherwise."

Chapter 41

The fairies gathered on the dark coastline and laid their open video clip phone watches on the sand encountering up. The video enjoys developed an ideal line as the light illuminated all their faces. The elves aligned throughout the beach with Barnabas standing in front. They looked worn out and beat.

" Everyone ready?" Barnabas stated. With that said he struck a remote control button in his hand which turned all the video clip enjoys on in record mode.

" Santa, get right here soon. It has actually worsened by the min, and I'm uncertain just how much longer we can take it," he stated.

The elves then chanted in unison, "Send out assistance!"

Barnabas clicked the push-button control button turning off the video clip watches. "The message is on the way," he stated.

Chapter 42

It was dark outdoors as Eric stood in the dimly lit garage looking at Santa's Mini Cooper sleigh. He could not withstand running his turn over the exterior.

" She's an appeal isn't she?" Santa claimed from the garage interior door."

" It reminds me of my childhood. The expectancy of listening to a smack on the roof covering. Just how were you able to do this year after year?" Eric asked.

" I have actually done it since it has actually been my honor to spread pleasure. Not everybody can be Santa. I simply hope the fairies don't dislike me."

" They know you care. I hope I have not dissatisfied you considering that we have not obtained the North Post or the fairies back."

" What do you suggest? You are doing an exceptional work."

" I love collaborating with you, and also wish I can see this project with throughout."

" Is it something that I did?"

" No, Santa. You have been an absolute delight. I'm just attempting to stabilize my work life and also my individual life."

" I see."

" I am mosting likely to recommend another person who can complete the job. I have actually prayed to discover an answer, but there is only one solution."

" You require to be with your household. I'm a huge kid. I can take care of myself."

" Thanks you for understanding."

" You have actually established me on the ideal path and for that I am for life thankful."

Chapter 43

Santa looked extremely dispirited as he beinged in the stiff chair of Stanislov's law office. The only light on his face was from his video clip phone watch. The sun was simply coming to a head over the perspective.

" Hi, Mom."

" Papa, you look terrible. What's wrong?" Mrs. Claus asked.

" My army has actually decreased even more. I'm down to Stanislov as well as Freddy helping me out."

" I am so sorry. I believed there was potential there." "Me also."

" More bad news. You obtained an email from a little girl asking if you were going to go to the opening of the most recent The Santa Company store."

" Where is this one?" Santa asked.

" Regarding four blocks from you at the Hudson and also Marshall store."

Santa switched off his video clip phone and also got his boots. He trudged down the pathway and also made his way to the department store. Arrows outside pointed to the stores rotating door. Santa pushed his means through the door and more arrowheads directed buyers to the Christmas Store. Santa strolled through the store just taking a short stop at a fashion jewelry display case to appreciate the hanging pocket watches.

Decors draped the wall surfaces of the Christmas Store. Santa's chair as well as workshop rested at the center of the area. Currently moms and dads with their youngsters lined up to satisfy Santa. Helga and also CG oversaw the shop elves. Numerous of the extremely thrilled youngsters spotted Santa.

" Santa! Santa! Over right here!" one of the kids screamed. The child desperately waved at Santa.

" Santa! My kid wishes to sit in your lap," one of the moms and dads bellowed.

Now in the turmoil Helga finally found Santa. "Just how type of you to join us. I didn't understand you were coming," she said.

" I intended to talk in person with you and also see this sham with my own eyes," Santa said.

" Do you desire me to have him removed?" CG asked. "No, that will not be required," Helga responded.

As Helga grabbed Santa's arm to guide him to a peaceful spot to talk, she slipped a hanging watch right into Santa's jacket pocket. CG followed them to their silent spot.

" You are eliminating the fairies and also destroying the spirit of Xmas," Santa said

"I don't assume you can know that since we took away all their video clip phones," Helga said.

"Just how useless," Santa stated.

"And we're doing exactly what we promised," she said. "Bringing good will as well as cheer," CG said.

"At the suffering of the fairies. I guarantee you I will obtain them back," Santa stated.

"And also I guarantee you this. The only method to do that is if I'm 6 feet under, as well as they are disposing dust on my head," Helga said.

Santa stepped back, completely shocked.

"Time for you to run along now. The actual Santa will certainly be coming out that door in five, 4, three, 2, one," CG counted.

The workshop door opened with fantastic excitement as the store's Santa got in the workshop.

"Ho! Ho! Ho! Merry Christmas!" the shop Santa said. He held his round belly which shook like a dish filled with jelly.

The group of parents as well as kids pushed onward in line to get a better sight of the shop Santa. The security personnel held the group back as store Santa made his means to his chair.

There was an unexpected scream. "Protection! Security!" Helga shouted. "We have a thief," as she indicated the actual Santa Claus.

The security personnel promptly ordered Santa and restrained him. "Look! He has a stolen watch in his pocket," Helga stated.

The security personnel reached right into Santa's layer pocket as well as took out the same watch Santa had actually appreciated previously in the precious jewelry case.

"I did not put that there," Santa stated. "Then just how did it arrive?" Helga asked. "I don't know," Santa claimed.

"Take him to the security office and also call the cops," Helga demanded.

The security guards flaunted Santa out of the workshop before all the parents and also shocked kids..

Chapter 44

Santa paced back and forth in his cell as a police offer came over to open the lock.

"You are free to go," the police officer said.

"Did someone post bail?"

"Yes, your attorney did. He's waiting in the lobby."

"Thank heavens."

Santa and Stanislov walked down the block and crossed the street to Stanislov's office. Inside, Santa collapsed onto a leather couch.

"I was set up. I know that watch was planted on me, but I can't prove it."

"Your problems are only getting worse. The press has dubbed you Clepto Claus." Stanislov dropped an open newspaper onto the desk. The front page featured a picture of Santa being put into a police car. The headline read "Clepto Claus Steals Christmas."

"All the news channels are running stories on it."

"Oh, my."

"And this video footage went viral." Stanislov turned around his laptop and played a Bloobtube clip titled, "Santa Arrested." It was a clip of Santa being led away by the security guards.

"Is that the number of people who have looked at it?" Santa asked.

"Yes, five million and counting. And that is just since this morning."

"What am I going to do? I've got to rescue the elves. They're counting on me, and all I've done is let them down."

"I know they don't feel that way. First thing is to win the trial against The Santa Company, and you get the North Pole back."

Chapter 45

It was another hot and steamy day at the Topengo warehouse. Leslie was walking on the beach when the ground shook violently. She hit the ground until it stopped moving. Leslie grabbed her phone and dialed.

"Ms. Montclair, the situation here is dangerous! All these quakes have caused equipment to break."

Helga was staring out the window of her animal print decorated office in New York City. She stepped carefully onto the bear rug so as not to trip.

"Leslie, my darling. I suggest you fix it. Get the production numbers up or you will be looking for another job."

"Ms. Montclair, you don't understand how desperate we are. I'm more concerned for everyone's safety," Leslie said.

"Wrong! Wrong! Wrong!" Helga shouted into her phone. "That's why you will never get ahead in this company. Get those gifts flowing again or else." Helga slammed her phone down.

"What was all that about?" CG asked from the office door.

Helga pulled out a report from her desk drawer and threw it at CG's feet. CG bent down and picked it up. The top page bar graph chart shows the bars decreasing each month.

"Each time a video of Santa goes viral our orders drop because the sales have dropped," Helga said.

"Ouch. I didn't realize they were that low," CG said.

"Eliminating Santa will be a pleasure. I can't wait to see his little chubby face in court," Helga said.

CG excused himself from Helga and slipped into an empty office. He pulled out a letter from his pocket and opened it. The letterhead read "Swiss National Bank." The account was in the name of Cliff Grable. CG grabbed his phone.

"Accounting department did you get the invoices I sent over? They need to get paid today."

"Yes, sir," the accounting department said. "The money has already been wired."

"Thank you," CG said as he hung up the phone and smiled.

Chapter 46

A banged up Molly Ann ran in the front door of her home and looked around.

"Welcome home, Small Fry," Eric said.

"Santa! Santa!" Molly Ann yelled.

Kelly looked up the empty staircase. "He had very pressing business and had to leave us," he said.

"But he didn't say goodbye," Molly Ann said. "Daddy, did he fire you?"

"No, Small Fry. He did not fire me," Eric said. "We just came to a mutual understanding."

"It really is for the better," Kelly said.

"You always finish your jobs. You told me so," Molly Ann said. "You dumped Santa!"

"Honey, it is not like that at all. I have to take care of our family," Eric said. "And you are my first concern."

"It was just getting too crazy around here, and we didn't want to see you get hurt again," Kelly said.

"He trusted you and you sold him out," Molly Ann said as she ran down the hall and into her bedroom, followed by a very loud door slam.

"Give her some time and she will be OK," Kelly said.

"I just hope Santa is," Eric said.

Chapter 47

The next morning Molly Ann sat in front of her mirror brushing her hair to make sure that it covered up the bruise on her forehead. She put her brush down and grabbed her Hello Kitty Piggy Bank and put it into her backpack.

"Molly Ann, hurry up. You're going to be late for school," Kelly yelled from downstairs.

"I'll be down in a second." Molly Ann said as she studied the city bus routes on her computer.

"Don't dally," Kelly yelled.

Molly Ann grabbed her backpack and headed out of her room.

Chapter 48

News crews stalked the steps of the courthouse. Half the crowd carried signs supporting Santa while the other half of the crowd carried signs denouncing Santa. Local news reporter, Wally Rafferty, was dressed in a suit and tie and had his black hair poofed up as high as it could go.

"We are here at court for Santa versus The Santa Company," Wally said. "Both parties are counter suing each other."

As Santa, Stanislov and Freddy exited their car, reporters swamped them.

"Santa, what do you hope to get out of this trial?" Wally asked.

"We are here to prove that Santa was swindled out of the North Pole," Stanislov said.

"Santa, any comments?" Wally asked.

"I want everyone to know how badly The Santa Company is treating the elves. My goal is to get them to the North Pole where they are safe," Santa said.

"Any word for your fans?" Wally asked.

"It is good to see that people still believe in me, and I did not shoplift. Keep the faith," Santa said.

"No more questions," Stanislov said. "We are due inside."

Stanilsov and Freddy ushered Santa past the crowds and into the courthouse just as Helga and crew exited their car.

"Ms. Montclair, why are you here?" Wally asked.

"Santa has financially derailed our company. I want to see him get what he deserves," she said.

"So you are blaming Santa for your demise?" Wally asked.

"Yes. If it weren't for Santa's shenanigans, The Santa Company wouldn't be bankrupt," CG said.

"Any final comments" Wally asked.

"I'm going to sit in the front row and watch Santa go down," Helga said. She turned as the crowd parted in front of her as she went up the courthouse steps.

Chapter 49

The station wagon pulled up to the curbside drop off at Molly Ann's school. Students walked by and the crossing guard waved students across the street.

Kelly turned to Molly Ann. "Are you sure you're ready to go back to school?

"Yes, Pa Pop," Molly Ann said.

"Here's your lunch," Kelly said as he passed Molly Ann the brown paper bag lunch. "If at any time you don't feel comfortable, have your teacher call me. They have my cell."

"OK. At least the boys said they were sorry."

"Accidents do happen. I love you, Sweetie. Have a good day."

"Pa Pop, you know Santa didn't mean to cause any problems."

"Honey, don't worry about that. Everything is fine now."

Kelly reached across the front seats of the station wagon and hugged Molly Ann.

"I love you too," Molly Ann said as she exited the minivan.

Molly Ann meandered up the front stairs of the school as the station wagon drove away. Instead of going in she grabbed a seat on a bench in the schoolyard as it emptied out. The interior school bell rang, and Molly Ann took her opportunity. She stood up and put on her backpack. She ran to the bus stop as the city bus approached, and then stopped. The city bus doors popped open. Molly Ann walked up the stairs with her change for the bus in her hand.

"Little girl, aren't you a little young to be out here by yourself?" the bus driver asked.

"No, ma'am. I missed the class bus trip to the courthouse so I'm heading down there to rejoin my class," Molly Ann said.

"You're lucky. I will drop you off right in front. Put your money in the meter and take the seat right here behind me. I will tell you when it is your stop," the bus driver said.

Molly Ann grabbed her seat and clutched her backpack.

Chapter 50

Santa, Stanislov and Freddy huddled at the defendant's table inside the courtroom. Suddenly, the back doors of the courtroom opened and Helga, CG and their three lawyers entered. They all walked in unison to their table.

The bailiff called the court to order. "This court is now in session with the honorable Judge Westmoreland presiding."

The studious judge entered the courtroom from her chambers.

"Both parties will present their case, and then I will make a decision. Stanislov, please make your opening statement," Judge Westmoreland commanded.

"We will show that the contract Santa signed was not the complete contract and part of the agreement was removed by The Santa Company," he said.

"The Santa Company, please make your opening statement," Judge Westmoreland ordered.

"We will show that the contract signed by Mr. Claus was the complete contract as submitted to The Santa Company," Lawyer 2 said.

"Santa's public appearances irreparably damaged the image of our client causing huge financial losses," Lawyer 1 said.

"The Santa Company owns the image to Santa Claus, and is seeking a judgment to prevent Santa Claus from making any public appearances," Lawyer 3 said.

The judge addressed Stanislov, "Stanislov, please call your first witness."

"We would like to call Britney Montgomery to the stand," Stanislov said.

Britney, from the TV studio in Toledo, walked up from the gallery and took her seat in the witness stand.

"We have all seen the video of Santa Claus naming you incorrectly. That was you in the video correct? Stanislov asked.

"Yes, it was," Britney said. "And I can tell you it was a day that changed my life forever."

"And how is that?" Stanislov asked.

"Santa knew I was adopted. The hospital said my birth mother had named me Britney, and my adopted parents decided to keep that name," Britney said. "They weren't aware that my birth mother has actually named me Amy."

"She was probably born in a barn!" Helga shouted.

"Quiet in the courtroom," Judge Westmoreland said as she banged her gavel. "Please continue."

"I found out there was a mix-up on the birth certificate. Knowing that I was able to find my birth mother," Britney said.

"Anything you would like to say to Santa?" Stanislov asked.

"I cannot thank you enough. Santa is the real deal."

"You may step down," the judge said.

Britney stepped down from the witness box and went over to the defendant's table and gave Santa a great big hug.

Chapter 51

Cathy Miller, the school secretary, sat at her desk chewing on a pencil. She shuffled the morning attendance sheets. The absentee sheet showed that Molly Ann was absent, but she hadn't received a call from the Thorsens letting the school know she wouldn't be in attendance today. She picked up her desk phone and dialed.

"Hi, Mr. Thorsen, this is Cathy Miller. I was calling to see why Molly Ann wasn't in school today. Is she not feeling well?"

Kelly looked his phone in shock.

"What do you mean Molly Ann isn't there? I dropped her off myself this morning."

"Mr. Thorsen, I'm looking over the homeroom attendance sheets and Molly Ann is not here," Miss Miller said.

"Can you please check that to make sure it is correct?" Kelly asked.

"I did. Her teacher confirmed she was not in homeroom this morning."

"Oh my God. Please call the police," Kelly instructed the school secretary. He hung up the phone and immediately dialed again.

"Eric, Molly Ann is missing. Please get home."

Chapter 52

In the courtroom, Stanislav called John Sweeney, the ice rink manager, to the witness stand.

"Mr. Sweeney, please tell the judge how you came to meet Santa Claus?" Stanislov asked.

"At the Ice Capades show in our arena. He was able to save the show by refreezing the ice," Mr. Sweeney said.

"And he was escorted from the building," Helga interjected.

"I will only say this once," Judge Westmoreland said. "Control your client or I will hold her in contempt. Continue."

"And the video of that was posted on Bloobtube?" Stanislov continued.

"The tech who filmed it posted it, and it just took off," Mr. Sweeney said.

"Santa had nothing to do with posting the video?

"Correct. Mr. Sweeney said. "He made me a believer again, and I am now filled with Christmas spirit year round."

"Thank you. No more questions," Stanislov said as he dismissed the witness.

John Sweeney stood up and exited the witness box, and he, too, made his way over to the defendant's table and hugged Santa. He headed out the back doors of the courtroom just as Molly Ann entered.

"We are going to take a ten minute recess," Judge Westmoreland said as she banged her gavel.

As Santa stood up from the table he saw Molly Ann in the back of the courtroom and waved to her.

Chapter 53

As Eric and Kelly pulled into the school parking lot news broke on the radio.

"In business news, The Santa Company has filed for bankruptcy protection. More news as the story develops," the dj said.

Several police cars were already parked there. Cathy Miller and Cassie spoke with the officers as Eric and Kelly approached.

"Have you found her?" Eric asked.

"Not yet Mr. Thorsen," Cathy said.

"Cassie, did Molly Ann say anything to you about where she might go?" Kelly asked.

"No, she didn't say a word," Cassie said.

Chapter 54

Molly Ann ran joyfully down the center aisle of the courtroom to Santa, who grabbed her and gave her a very tight hug.

"I thought I would never see you again!" Molly Ann said. "You left without saying goodbye."

"I shouldn't have," Santa said. "How is that bump on your head?"

"It's better. Look, the bruising is almost gone." Molly Ann lifted up her bangs to show Santa that the bruises had faded.

"Such a brave girl. Where are your parents?

"At home."

"How did you get here?"

"By bus. The city bus stops right our front."

"Your parents don't know you're here?"

"No, I didn't want them to get into another fight about you."

"They must be worried to death. Stanislov, let me borrow your phone. Everything will be all right."

It's OK. They always kiss and make up," Molly Ann said.

Chapter 55

In the school parking lot, Eric felt his phone ringing in his pocket. He pulled it out and looked at the caller ID. It was Stanislov calling.

"Stainslov?" Eric asked.

"No, Eric. It's Santa."

"Santa, I don't have time to talk right now. Molly Ann's missing."

"No, she isn't. She's here at the courthouse."

Eric took a deep breath.

"Who is it? Is it Molly Ann?" Kelly asked.

"It's Santa. Molly Ann is with him."

"With Santa? Isn't he at court?"

"Yes, come on let's get over there."

Chapter 56

The court recess was over, and Judge Westmoreland slid behind the bench as Molly Ann was now seated in the front row behind Santa.

"The Santa Company, please present your case," Judge Westmoreland said.

Lawyer 2 got up from the plaintiff's table and approached the Judge.

"They have no proof that the contract is not valid," Lawyer 2 said. "And each time a video was posted the sales at The Santa Company decreased."

"By millions and millions," Helga interjected.

"Ms. Montclair, do you need to be removed?" Judge Westmoreland asked.

"No, your Honor," Helga said.

"Stanislov, what do you have to say?" Judge Westmoreland asked.

As the Judge finished her question, Eric and Kelly crept into the courtroom, trying not to disturb anyone, but Molly Ann heard the courtroom doors open. She stood up on her seat and waved to her dads. Eric and Kelly ran up front and both wrapped their arms around Molly Ann.

"Please sit down," Judge Westmoreland said.

"The portion of the contract protecting the elves was removed by an elf working for The Santa Company," Stanislov said.

"Then get him on the stand," Judge Westmoreland said.

"We can't," Stanislov replied.

"And the videos?" Judge Westmoreland asked.

"The videos were posted by fans. Santa had no knowledge of them," Stanislov said.

"Even if he didn't realize it at the time, Santa did sign away his rights to his image," Judge Westmoreland said as she held up the signature page of the contract. "Is this his signature?"

"Yes."

"Unfortunately I have no proof that Santa signed this contract under false pretenses. I am ruling in favor of The Santa Company," Judge Westmoreland said.

"Come on, Judge," Stanislov said.

"Santa Claus is hereby prohibited from making public appearances as Santa Claus," Judge Westmoreland ruled.

Helga and CG jumped for joy and hugged at the plaintiff's table. The rest of the crowd sat in utter silence, looking shocked.

"I'm sorry, Small Fry," Eric said. "I let you down."

"Daddy, this can't happen to Santa," Molly Ann said. "You always take care of the small things."

"Say that again," Eric said.

"You always take care of the small things," Molly Ann repeated.

"Stanislov, stop her before she bangs her gavel," Eric said. "I've got an idea."

"Judge, please one minute," Stanislov asked.

"Once I bang the gavel the decision is final."

Eric jumped up to the table. He grabbed the contract and quickly searched through it.

"Small things. It's all about the small things," Eric said. "Every contract has some fine print. Look for the fine print."

Freddy, Stanislov and Santa held up the last page of the contract. A small line was barely visible at the bottom of the page.

"Oh my God. Freddy said elf Marty was a contract genius. Does anyone have a magnifying glass?"

"Here, I have an app on my phone for that," Eric said.

Freddy hooked the phone to a laptop and projector. He held the phone over the bottom of the page. The projector displayed the bottom line on the courtroom screen.

"In Case Of Bankruptcy All Properties Will Revert To The Original Owner, Santa Claus."

"No! No! No!" CG and Helga screamed.

"Judge, since The Santa Company has filed for bankruptcy, we ask you to reconsider your decision," Stanislov said.

"Based on this evidence, I rule in favor of Santa Claus, and all North Pole properties belong to you again," Judge Westmoreland said as she banged her gavel.

The crowd exploded in screams and shouts, and people hugged everyone around them.

At that moment a very official person walked up the center aisle with two police officers in tow.

"Judge, I'm Tony Roemmele with the US Bankruptcy Court. I'm here to arrest Helga Montclair and Cliff Grable," he said.

“Me, under arrest? What forever for?” Helga asked.

“For Embezzlement. An audit of the books show that you have been skimming money off the top for months now,” Mr. Roemmele said.

“How could you, Helga?” CG said.

“Don’t act so innocent,” Mr. Roemmele said. “You had your own scheme going. You both are guilty of running the company into the ground.”

“Officers, please place these two under arrest,” Judge Westmoreland said.

“I thought you would be in jail by now after I put that watch in your pocket,” Helga said and quickly grabbed her mouth as she let the cat out of the bag.

“Finally the proof to clear your name one hundred percent,” Eric said.

“Judge, is that enough to get the shoplifting charge dropped?” Stanislov asked.

“I will speak to the DA to have the charges dropped,” Judge Westmoreland said.

Helga and CG were handcuffed and escorted out of the courtroom by the two police officers.

“Eric, thank you for saving me and the North Pole,” Santa said.

Santa and his entire team left the courtroom and headed out. Outside, it was a beautiful day.

On the courthouse steps Eric bent down onto one knee. He looked Molly Ann directly in the eyes. “Molly Ann, never do that again. You gave me and your Pa Pop a huge scare.”

“I just wanted to see Santa,” she said. “I didn’t get a chance to say goodbye.”

“Santa, I was wrong,” Kelly said. “I never should have told Eric to stop working with you. He is a good man and believes in you.”

“I never doubted that for a minute,” Santa said.

Kelly and Eric kissed and hugged.

“See? They always make up,” Molly Ann said.

“Good. Now let’s go get the elves,” Santa said.

Chapter 57

At the South Pole Mrs. Claus looked at the wall of video screens. An elf who secretly kept a video watch was able to send a video to Santa. It was a volcano that spewed ash down on the warehouse and covered the beach and pier. Suddenly, a call from Santa came in. Santa's face was spread out over the video screens to form one image of Santa.

"Mama, get the Santabagos and meet me in Topengo. We've got to pull the elves off that island now."

"I'll meet you there with help. The conditions are really deteriorating there."

"God speed. I love you!"

Chapter 58

Inside the Thorsen's garage Santa put the harness on Dasher. Eric mounted the Ice Maker Ray Gun TX on to the sleigh's front hood. Kelly and Molly Ann packed the sleigh.

"Santa, as a family we want to go with you and help," Eric said.

"I don't want to put your family in danger," Santa said.

"Santa, you are family, and family helps family out," Kelly said.

"Yeah!" Molly Ann said.

"Thank you. Let's go," Santa said.

Santa, Eric, Molly Ann and Kelly jumped into the Mini-Cooper sleigh. Santa grabbed the reins.

"Fasten your seat belts. On Dasher!" Santa commanded.

Dasher pulled the sleigh with ease, and within an instant they were airborne. Dasher and the sleigh rose quickly to cruising altitude at supersonic speed. A full moon lit the night sky as Molly Ann rested her head against Kelly, who pulled a blanket over both of them as they settled in for the flight to Topengo.

The morning sun rose as Barnabas and Leslie gathered all the elves on the pier. Ash fell down and large chunks of rocks flew through the air and crashed into the bay, causing large waves that slammed against the pier, soaking the elves.

In the distance, the Santabago, piloted by Mrs. Claus could be seen coming over the horizon.

"Come in, Big Red. This is Mama Jingle," she said into the radio.

"Come in, Mama Jingle," Santa said back.

"The Santabago has sleigh blades. There are too many rocks on the beach now, so I can't land on the sand. We're stacked up here because I've got the Santabago II right on my tail," Mrs. Claus said. Just then a flaming ball of rock flew by her window.

"Circle till we get there. We're almost there," Santa said on the radio.

In the Mini-Cooper Sleigh Santa put his plans into action.

"Kelly, reach behind your seat and pull out the red bag," Santa said.

Kelly pulled out a large red bag that had a rope tie. He handed the bag to Santa. "What's in there?" he asked.

"It's the bubble gun and the Elf Tracker," Eric said.

"Dasher, aim for the harbor. We only get one shot at this. There's the island," Santa said pointing to the smoke cloud that spread above the island. The other Santabagos could be seen circling the island.

Santa grabbed the radio microphone. "Mama Jingle, give us a little clearance and fall in behind us. We are going to lay some ice,"

"Roger that. Falling in behind you," Mrs. Claus said on the radio.

"Here we go Dasher," Santa said.

Dasher nodded and increased speed to get in front of the other two Santabagos. They all formed a single line. Santa checked all the gauges on the Mini-Cooper sleigh. Everything looked good.

"Eric, when I tell you, hit this button," Santa said, and pointed to the large TX button.

"Understood," Eric said.

"Make sure your seat belts are fastened tight, because here we go," Santa said.

The Mini-Cooper sleigh took a steep dive over the water to get low to enter the harbor. As it entered the harbor, it leveled off and headed for the water near the beach.

"Hit the button now!" Santa yelled.

Eric hit the button and immediately a wide, blue beam of light hit the water. The water froze into a thick, wide sheet of ice instantly which extended all the way to the pier.

The elves all cheered at the sight of Santa Claus.

"It's going to be a little bumpy, so hold tight," Santa said.

Dasher took the Mini-Cooper sleigh down onto the ice sheet. It bumped and bucked and finally skidded to a stop by the pier. Santa, Eric and Kelly hopped out, to the cheers of the elves.

"Molly Ann, stay here," Kelly said.

"Yes, Pa Pop," she replied.

Mrs. Claus followed the same path that Santa took and landed her Santabago on the sheet of ice, quickly followed by the Santabago II. The elves scrambled down the pier to the sheet of ice and rushed to their rides. The flaming rocks fell as Santa, Eric and Kelly rounded up the elves and put them into the Santabagos.

"Eric, use the bubble gun. Shoot it at the elves. It will give them temporary protection from the falling rocks," Santa said.

Eric pulled out the bubble gun from the red bag and started shooting at the elves. Giant bubbles enveloped the elves, which were strong enough to bounce the rocks away from them

Mrs. Claus stood at the door of the Santabago, trying to stay calm, but still yelling to the elves, "Get in here! Hurry!"

Santa pulled out his Elf Tracker to make sure all the elves made it to the Santabagos. There was still one dot on the tracker showing an elf in the warehouse.

"Eric, get your family into one of the Santabagos. I need the bubble gun," Santa said.

"Let me come with you," Eric said.

"You have done enough," Santa said. "Please get everyone out of here. I'll be right behind you."

Santa turned the bubble gun on and enveloped himself in a protective bubble. He looked at the Elf Tracker and started to run to the burning warehouse.

Eric ran to the Mini-Cooper and gathered up Kelly and Molly Ann. They ran to the nearest Santabago, and once on board, the Santabgos took off as fast as they could.

Santa entered the burning warehouse as his temporary bubble popped. He looked for the remaining elf. Through the smoke and flames he made out the lone elf who stood in the distance with his back to Santa.

"Barnabas, time to go."

"No, Santa. I don't deserve to be saved. I have hurt so many people."

"You were doing what you thought was right. No one knew it would turn out like this. Barnabas, look at me."

Barnabas turned to face Santa as tears streamed down his cheeks.

"I can never make it up to them."

"Yes you can, by being my Head Elf. They still look up to you. Your actions will show them how much they mean to you."

"But Santa…"

"No buts. We have a big job ahead of us and only a short period of time to get it done." Santa extended his hand to Barnabas who grabbed onto it.

As they sprinted to get out of the burning warehouse, a beam fell and pinned them both to the floor. The beam crushed the bubble gun. Santa and Barnabas struggled under the weight of the beam. No matter what they did they couldn't lift the heavy beam, as more parts of the warehouse collapsed.

"Santa! Santa!" Eric screamed.

“Over here!” both Santa and Barnabas yelled as the smoke got thicker.

Eric rushed over and tried to lift one end of the beam to free them both. The weight was just too much.

“This is for everyone who believes in you!” Eric yelled.

He grabbed the beam, and with a rush of adrenaline the beam shifted. Santa and Barnabas pushed on the beam as Eric raised the beam even higher, giving them both room to slide out. Barnabas held his arm.

“You OK?” Eric asked.

“My arm,” Barnabas said.

“We’ll get it looked at, but now it’s time to run,” Eric said.

They made a mad dash, and exited the quickly disintegrating warehouse. Outside wasn’t any better, as more flaming rocks fell on the beach around them.

“Think of this as flaming dodge ball,” Eric said.

All three zig-zagged their way through the falling, flaming rocks as they ran to the Mini-Cooper sleigh. They dove into the Mini-Cooper as Santa gave the command to Dasher,” Go, Dasher, go!”

Dasher sprinted and took off on a very steep climb. Barnabas looked out the back window to see the volcano explode, sending down rocks and lava which covered the warehouse and the pier. The island was completely destroyed.

Chapter 59

Activity abounded at the North Pole. Outside the elves, trained the reindeer while others raced on the polar bears.

Inside, the bright faced and happy elves made toys. Barnabas, with his arm in a sling, inspected the work as the toys came off the assembly line. Santa, Eric, Molly Ann and Kelly watched from the balcony above.

"Will the toys be delivered on time?" Molly Ann asked.

"Yes, they will," Santa said.

"Santa, I am so sorry that I ever doubted you," Kelly said.

"Your faith was tested, but you did what was right for your family," Santa said.

"And family is everything. I'm so glad you believe again," Eric said as he hugged Kelly.

"Eric, you are the most sincere person I have ever met. There is not an ounce of ill will in your body," Santa said.

"So does this mean you're not retiring?" Molly Ann asked.

"Oh, I'm still retiring, but I have found a replacement," Santa said.

"Who?" Molly Ann asked.

From the loudspeakers there was a page for Santa, "Santa, please report to the Good Deeds Room. Santa to the Good Deeds Room."

Santa lead the way as Eric, Molly Ann and Kelly followed to the Good Deeds Room. Inside, elf Ian manned the Good Deeds Radar.

"Santa," elf Ian said, "When I started up the equipment I noticed that there was a burned out bulb on the radar." Elf Ian turned the machine off and then back on. All the bulbs on the radar lit up except for a burned out bulb over Toledo, Ohio.

"Every time I replace the bulb, it lights up and then blows out," elf Ian said as he pulled out the dead bulb and tossed it into the trash can.

"Elf Ian, replace it with a larger wattage bulb please," Santa said.

Elf Ian rummaged through a box of light bulbs and pulled out a much larger bulb that he screwed into the slot over Toledo, Ohio. This time the bulb burned very brightly while all the other bulbs on the radar went dark.

"Look Santa. The Good Deed signal. Right over Toledo," elf Ian said.

"Molly Ann, to answer your question, I have made my selection on who will replace me if he will have the job," Santa said and looked at Eric. Molly

Ann and Kelly both smiled at the news.

"Me? Are you sure? Eric asked.

"I have never been so sure of anything in my life. You have a big heart and patience. All the things that make a good Santa."

"How can I ever fill your shoes?" Eric asked.

"It is a learning process, and you have your family here to support you." An elf handed Santa a fresh Santa suit on a hanger. "Here, I believe this fits you," Santa said as he presented Eric with his own red Santa suit.

"This is an honor I will treasure for the rest of my life," Eric said as he hugged Santa and waved to Molly Ann and Kelly to join him in the group hug.

"Try it on," Santa said. Eric slipped on the red suit and tightened up the belt. "Looks like you have some extra room in your suit, but you are missing one thing." Santa took off his hat and placed it on Eric's head. "Now the look is complete."

"I have never been more proud," Kelly said.

"Can I put in my toy request now?" Molly Ann asked.

The entire group laughed at the request.

"Let's announce this to the elves," Santa said. "They are all waiting downstairs."

Santa led the group as the Thorsen family walked hand in hand to the balcony where Mrs. Claus was waiting and clapping.

The End